To Pat
and he

Enjoy —
Sheila Benech

TO OUR
CHILDREN'S
CHILDREN

# TO OUR CHILDREN'S CHILDREN

*Preserving Family Histories for Generations to Come*

## BOB GREENE
*and D. G. Fulford*

DOUBLEDAY
NEW YORK   LONDON   TORONTO   SYDNEY   AUCKLAND

PUBLISHED BY DOUBLEDAY
a division of
Bantam Doubleday Dell Publishing Group, Inc.
1540 Broadway, New York, New York 10036

DOUBLEDAY and the portrayal of an anchor
with a dolphin are trademarks of Doubleday,
a division of Bantam Doubleday Dell Publishing Group, Inc.

*Book design by Patrice Fodero*

Library of Congress Cataloging-in-Publication Data

Greene, Bob and Fulford, D. G.
  To our children's children : preserving family histories for generations to
come / Bob Greene and D.G. Fulford. — 1st ed.
     p.   cm.
  1. Biography as a literary form.   2. Autobiography.   3. Oral
biography.   I. Fulford, D. G.   II. Title.
CT22.G74   1993
920.02—dc20                                                          92-29082
                                                                          CIP

ISBN 0-385-46797-4

Printed in the United States of America

March 1993

**12  14  16  18  20  19  17  15  13  11**

*For*
*our mother*
*and*
*our father*

# CONTENTS

# $\mathcal{T}$HIS BOOK AND YOU
## ❧

Welcome! We're glad that you decided to embark on this project, and we hope it turns out to be one of the most satisfying things you've ever done.

You will find in these pages many questions— questions to lead you down the pathways of your own life. What you're going to be doing is putting together a personal history for your family. We're here to show you that it can be easy and full of pleasure for you—something intimate and special, the creating of a lasting and beautiful hand-me-down for your children, your children's children, and generations that will come along far in the future.

Your story will have much more resonance for your children and grandchildren than any biography or autobiography of a famous person. It's almost startling that making this kind of personal history hasn't always been an American custom. Older people are often able to leave property or money behind for their descendants, but this—a package of memories of a person's life—is what usually doesn't get passed along. The most precious commodities of all—people's own recollections of their worlds—seldom get preserved, at least in a proper and permanent way.

As you will see, the secret of all this is found in the particulars. The specifics of your own memories are what your family will treasure the most. The main thing for you to know is that you need not attempt to sum up your life in grand, sweeping historic strokes, but stick to the seemingly small basics.

Thus, a man in his seventies shouldn't try to tell his children what post–World War I America was like; he should answer for them the question "What did the neighborhood where you grew up look like?" Or: "Who was your best friend when you were a boy, and what did the two of you do together?" Or: "How did you get your first job, and what was it like on your first day?"

A woman in her eighties shouldn't try to reconstruct the political events that took place during her youth. She should reach into her memory to answer questions on richer topics: "What was your schoolhouse like?" Or: "What do you remember about going on automobile rides with your family?" Or: "Describe what you would do on summer days when you were a girl."

The purpose of this book is to help you along the

way. If you know what questions to ask yourself, the answers almost take care of themselves—you already know them, but you may not have thought about them in a while.

Maybe you have never considered that the stories from your life are important. But be assured that they will be cherished far beyond anything money could buy. Whether you write your history, or speak it into a tape recorder, your stories will be eagerly awaited by the most appreciative audience of all—your family. Far into the future, your family will read your words or listen to your voice and be grateful you took the time to put this gift together for them.

# GETTING STARTED

Some quick hints and pointers before you begin:

- The most important thing for you to keep in mind is that this is meant to be a pleasure to do, not a task to be completed. When you first flip through the book, it will look to you as if there are a million questions. You don't have to answer each one. In fact, if you chose just *one* question and answered it in the form of a note to your family, that in itself would surely please them. This is not a test. There are no correct or incorrect answers.

- Some people like to write their memories down, others like to talk them into a tape recorder. Choose which is more comfortable for you. If you decide to tape, you can do so at your leisure and then come back to the recorder and pick up where you left off last time. If you enjoy using pen and paper, don't feel as if you must sit down and write *Moby Dick* every day. Doing this in small bursts is fine. You may want to keep scratch pads by your bed and in the kitchen. Thoughts will come to you when you don't even know you're thinking about the project.

- You aren't working on deadline. Take your time. If you plan to give your children your memories as a gift for a certain holiday, allow yourself plenty of time to do the project to your satisfaction. Perhaps you may want to make appointments with yourself to work on it. Don't rush— allow yourself time to savor the process. Look through old family papers and photographs. They will jog your memory; memories beget memories. Give your mind a chance to ramble.

- This can be a very private process. When you work on it, you may want to go to a quiet place where you can be by yourself. Or, if you choose to share the project with your spouse, that's an idea that can work well. The two of you will have a good time talking about things together. If you don't feel like letting anyone know what you're working on, let the machine answer the phone; tell your friends that you're out for a walk. Make this a time that you look forward to. So that this does not begin to feel like a job, schedule breaks for yourself in the middle of your writing or recording—lunch, a phone call, reading the day's mail.

- Don't ever worry whether your writing is interesting enough. It is.

- You'll see that some of the questions don't apply to you. Several are more for women, several others are more for men. Some may strike you as just plain silly. You don't have to answer them all —in fact, no one would probably want to try answering them all. Skip around if you want; don't keep track of how many you're answering. You don't have to complete a required percentage to be done. You're not being scored; you're finished when you're finished.

- To emphasize that last point again: Think of the questions as a menu. Choose which ones you want to address yourself to, and which ones you can do without. Just as you'd never think of ordering every item on a restaurant's menu, you should choose the questions here that pique your interest and your memories the most. If you don't feel like going on one day, once you've gotten started, quit for that day. Walk away and come back another time. This is not something to be endured, but to be enjoyed.

- Don't ever underestimate just how grateful your family will be that you're making the effort to do this for them. Think about how much you would have cherished it had your parents or grandparents answered a list of questions like these for you.

- Some questions seem like they are asking for a yes-or-no answer, but the purpose of every question in the book is to get you thinking and remembering. There's no right or wrong way to answer a specific question. The questions are to help you recall the times you've been through, the people you've known, and the places you've gone. If the question is a simple "What was your favorite flavor of ice cream?", your answer may be not only "Chocolate," but a story about the ice cream parlor you used to visit as a child— where it was, what it looked like, how you felt when you went there. Once you get going on a question, the form your answer takes is completely up to you.

- No detail is unimportant. The smallest things make up the richness of the big picture. Remembering what your parents' wallpaper looked like may set off a flood of other memories. And don't worry if some of these minuscule memories escape you—there are more than enough questions that will send your mind rushing back. You'll find that you remember more than you would have guessed.

- The first section of questions—"Facts," the section you are about to turn to—is purposely simple. It's a good way to get your feet wet, and to get started on the project. Leaf through the book and get comfortable with it. Then dive in. Once you've answered a few questions, you'll find yourself eager to keep going.

Have fun—this is your life.

# FACTS

### 1.

What is your name?

### 2.

Are you male or female?

### 3.

What is your address?

### 4.

What state were you born in? What city? What hospital?

### 5.

How old are you? What is your birthdate?

### 6.

What are your parents' names?

### 7.

Do you speak any foreign languages?

**8.**

What's your astrological sign?

**9.**

Are you right-handed or left-handed?

**10.**

Are you near-sighted or far-sighted?

**11.**

Are you overweight or underweight?

**12.**

What is your height, your weight, your eye color?

**13.**

Do you wear corrective lenses?

**14.**

What is your Social Security number?

**15.**

Are you married, divorced, or widowed?

**16.**

What was your maiden name?

### 17.
What is your spouse's name?

### 18.
What is your anniversary date? How many years have you been married?

### 19.
How many children do you have? How many grandkids? What are their names? How old are they?

### 20.
What is, or was, your occupation?

### 21.
Who is your next of kin?

### 22.
What is your race? What is your religion?

### 23.
What is your political affiliation?

### 24.
Do you live in the suburbs or in the city?

### 25.

Do you live in an apartment, a house, a condo, or a retirement home?

### 26.

Are you allergic to anything?

### 27.

What's your blood type?

### 28.

What does your voice sound like?

### 29.

What have been the names of your pets?

### 30.

What is your nickname?

# YOUR FAMILY AND ANCESTRY

ഔ

### 1.

What was your mother's name? Your father's name? Your grandmothers' names? Your grandfathers' names? What did you call them?

### 2.

Were they born in America? If not, where were they born? What circumstances brought them to the place where you were born? Were there people already there whom they knew, or did they come into the community alone? Was the community welcoming to them?

### 3.

Do you have brothers and sisters? What are their names? How old were you when they were born? Do you remember the first time you saw them?

### 4.

What about your aunts and uncles? What did they look like? Did they play an important part in your growing up? Did the family get together much casually, or did you have to travel and dress up to spend time together?

### 5.

Do you remember any special aunts and uncles? Was there someone your family was particularly proud of? Was there anyone of whom your family was not so proud?

### 6.

Was yours a religious family? Did you all attend services together? Were these dress-up affairs?

### 7.

What did your dad do for a living? Your mom? Your grandparents?

### 8.

Did you play with your cousins?

### 9.

Did your family take vacations? Did you go to the same place every year; a summer house or resort?

### 10.

Do you remember any special stories your grandmother or grandfather told you? Did you sit on a lap when you heard these stories, or side by side on the couch, or did you hear them when you and your grandparent were walking hand-in-hand, taking a stroll? Do you tell any of the same stories to your grandkids?

### 11.

What was your parents' relationship like? Would you describe it as warm? Formal? Loving? Stern? Demonstrative? Stereotypically male/female, or more unusual and equitable?

### 12.

Who were you named for? If it was a relative, did that make you feel especially close to that person, or did it put undue pressure on you?

### 13.

Did your grandparents live nearby? How often did you visit their homes? Did the house have a special cooking smell? Onions? Cookies? What did their couch feel like? How big was the kitchen?

### 14.

Did your family ever have a reunion? Did you meet any relatives there you had heard a lot about but didn't know?

### 15.

As a teenager, did you get along well with your parents, or was there trouble? How about your brothers and sisters? Did someone in your family cause your folks more trouble than the rest?

### 16.

Do you remember ever playing a trick on your brother or sister? Did you ever hurt their feelings when you really didn't mean to? What pictures come to mind when you think about playing together?

### 17.

Have your pets been like family members, or just like animals? Did you ever have a dog that ran away?

### 18.

List the pets you've had through the years. Where did you keep their feed dishes? Did you take them for walks, or was your time together less organized?

### 19.

Did your dad shave with a straight razor or an electric razor?

### 20.

Did your family pass down any superstitions?

### 21.

Did anyone in your family do handiwork? Needlework? Woodwork? Was anyone particularly mechanical?

### 22.

Did your family say grace? Did you sit down at the table together for every meal? Was it at the same time every day? Who sat where? What was the dinner table configuration?

### 23.

What did your father's handwriting look like? Your mother's?

### 24.

Were you considered rich, poor, or middle class? Were times ever tough for all of you, or was it always smooth sailing? Did you have to go without things that your friends had? Was this difficult for you? Who handled the money in your parents' house?

### 25.

Were your parents fancy dressers? When you think of them, what do you remember them wearing? Did your mother wear a special perfume you remember? Did she keep it in pretty bottles on her dresser? Did your father wear cologne or after-shave?

### 26.

Can you remember any stories you heard about your grandparents when they were children? Do you feel as if you knew much about their lives?

### 27.

What was it like when you took your spouse to meet your family? Were they welcoming or stand-offish? Was there one moment when you felt that your parents and siblings accepted your spouse as a family member?

### 28.

Do you have a piece of furniture or family heirloom that belonged to your parents or grandparents? What is it? Does it have a place of honor in your home?

### 29.

How did the Great Depression affect your family?

30.

When you think back on your mother and father now, what do you realize about their lives that you didn't understand when you were growing up?

31.

Looking back, do you think your parents were happy with the circumstances of their lives?

32.

Did your father have a favorite saying you can remember him repeating? How about your mother? Do you sometimes find their words coming out of your mouth?

# THE HOUSE OF YOUR GROWING UP

## 1.

What did your home look like? Was it a house or an apartment? What color was it? Was it stone or wood? One story or two?

## 2.

Can you remember the view out of any of your windows? What did you look out on? Your neighbors' houses? A row of stores? What stores? Or fields, woods, water, or mountains?

## 3.

What was your bedroom like? Did you share it with your siblings, or did you have it to yourself? Can you remember the carpeting, the wallpaper, the pictures that hung? What did you do to make it your own? Put pictures up of your favorite stars, paint the walls a certain color?

4.

What was your bed like? Your bedspread? Did you sleep with a stuffed animal or doll? What was your doll or animal's name?

5.

Can you remember what you daydreamed about as you looked out of your bedroom window?

6.

What time did the mail come? Can you remember getting anything in the mail that made you particularly excited?

7.

Did visitors knock at your door or ring a bell? What did it sound like? Did your parents keep the door locked, as people have to do now, or was it left unlatched for your comings and goings? How old were you when you were first trusted with a key?

8.

Did your family eat in the kitchen or in the dining room? What did the table settings look like?

### 9.

What do you remember having in the icebox when you were growing up? What would you see when you opened the icebox door?

### 10.

Who delivered to your house? A milkman? An iceman? A laundryman? An eggman? Or did you shop with your mother? At what kind of stores?

### 11.

What was your parents' room like? The beds, the bedspreads, the easy chairs? Did you spend much time in there with them? Were you allowed to rest in their beds when you were sick?

### 12.

Was there much music in your house? Did you listen to a radio or Victrola? Do you remember it being a quiet house or one filled with noise?

### 13.

Was there a lot of talking going on?

### 14.

Was there any place in your house that scared you? The basement? The attic? Or anyplace where you felt especially cozy, like halfway down the stairs?

15.

Did you have a lawn? Did you have flower beds? What kind of flowers did you grow? Did you help care for them; did you have chores?

16.

What was your favorite season at your house? Do you remember summer as too hot, or was it exhilarating and perfect? Did you have trees that flowered only at a certain time? Did ice and snow slow down your movement?

17.

Were there books in evidence around your house? Was there a special room in the house considered the "library"? Which of your parents' books do you remember reading? Which books do you remember them reading?

18.

Were your parents interested in the news? Which news stories made the greatest impression on you?

19.

What was the floor plan? Where were the telephones? How many bathrooms did you have? Did you have a shower or a bathtub?

### 20.

Did you have a back door or kitchen door? A side door? Which door did you come in most often?

### 21.

Who was there to greet you? Was your mother in the kitchen? Was your father in the living room?

### 22.

What time did you eat dinner? Was it at the same time every night? And who sat where?

### 23.

Were you proud of your house, or shy about having friends over?

### 24.

Did your parents have friends over often? Can you remember what their parties were like?

### 25.

Was your living room comfortable or formal? Is this where your family gathered for the most part, or did they gather in the kitchen or another room?

26.

What time of night do you remember your house getting quiet? Did your family stay up late or go to bed early?

27.

Did you eat breakfast together?

28.

Did company often come for meals?

29.

Did relatives or boarders live with your family? What were their quarters like? Were you allowed in there?

30.

Do you remember your house having a particular scent? Cooking smells or laundry smells or smells from your parents' work?

31.

What was the street like where you lived? Busy or quiet? Brick or paved? Was there a stoplight or stop sign on the corner?

### 32.

Did you have a fireplace? Did you sit around it often? Who built the fires at your house? What was the favored fire-starting method?

### 33.

How did you keep cool in the summertime? Window fans? Ceiling fans?

### 34.

Did you have a front stoop or a porch?

### 35.

Can you remember any major repairs your house needed? Did the roof leak? Did your family fix it or did you hire people to get it done? Or did it just stay that way for years?

### 36.

Can you remember your parents adding something they'd always wanted? A washing machine, maybe? A new icebox? An extra car?

### 37.

What was your address? Was it on your door? Your mailbox? Painted on the curb?

### 38.

Do you remember your phone number? Do you remember other phone exchanges in your town, before the switch to all-digit dialing?

### 39.

What magazines did your parents have around? What do you remember about the newspapers? Morning or evening or both? Who read which sections first?

### 40.

The first time you went away for more than a few days, what feeling went through you when you came back and caught sight of your house?

### 41.

If now, you could move back into the house you grew up in, just the way it was then, would you? Why, or why not?

# CHILDHOOD/NEIGHBORHOOD

### 1.

Who was your best friend in your neighborhood? Did you play at your homes, or mostly in the streets and playgrounds and fields? What do you remember about your friend's house? About your friend's family? Did you have a secret path you used to take to go to meet your friend?

### 2.

Did you play house? Who were you? The mother? The father? The family dog? Did you play stickball or sandlot baseball? What position did you play? Did the boys play together with the girls?

### 3.

Was there a neighborhood bully? Did he ever hurt you? What stories did you hear that made you think he was such a bad guy?

### 4.

Did you have a nickname?

### 5.

What sidewalk games did you play? If you jumped rope, do you remember any rhymes?

### 6.

Did you collect anything? Bugs, baseball cards, marbles, china figurines?

### 7.

Did you have pets? What were their names? Do you remember when they came to live with you? Do you remember how they died?

### 8.

Did you have chores around your house? Did you have to mow the lawn? Rake the leaves? Did you baby-sit for neighborhood kids? Did anything unusual happen while you were baby-sitting?

### 9.

Do you remember having the chicken pox, mumps, or any other childhood diseases? Were you ever seriously ill as a child? How did your mother take care of you?

### 10.

How was your neighborhood lit? Street lamps, porch lights?

### 11.

How did you go downtown and get back home? Car, trolley, walk, horseback? Can you remember your first trip downtown?

### 12.

Did you ever have a flood, tornado, or big snowstorm where you lived?

### 13.

Describe your neighborhood. Was it rural or suburban? Was it green or concrete?

### 14.

Did anyone in your neighborhood have a fancy garden? A horse? A gazebo? A tree you liked to climb?

### 15.

Did you go to the library?

### 16.

Do you remember a new family moving into your neighborhood? What was it like when you met them? Did your family welcome them by bringing food? Were they hard to make friends with? Did they join your circle?

17.

What were your favorite board games?

18.

Did you ever go door-to-door trying to sell anything to your neighbors? Did you have a lemonade
stand?

19.

Where did you go swimming?

20.

Did you move from your neighborhood? How did
that feel?

21.

Would you like to have raised your kids in a neighborhood like the one you grew up in? Why? Why
not?

22.

What was the name of your favorite doll?

23.

Did you have an imaginary friend when you were
growing up? Do you remember its name? How did
you picture it; as an animal or a child? Were your

parents aware of your imaginary life? Did they play along?

### 24.

Were you afraid of the boogeyman or the monster under the bed? What did your parents do to stop those fears?

### 25.

Do you remember your favorite bedtime story or poem? What one do you remember your parent reading to you? Which one do you remember reading to yourself?

### 26.

Did you go to camp? Were you homesick? Did anyone from your neighborhood go, too? Do you remember any counselors, or the names of any of your teams or activity groups?

### 27.

What did you ever do that got you in trouble at home? How did your parents discipline you?

### 28.

Did you have a swing set in your yard? A sandbox?

### 29.

Did you attend religious school?

### 30.

Was your neighborhood a good place in which to just walk around?

### 31.

What delivery trucks made regular stops on your block?

### 32.

Did you ever want to run away? Why?

### 33.

What was a perfect day when you were a child?

### 34.

What is your first memory? Crawling around the floor of your house? Sitting with your parents at dinner? Seeing a picture on the wall?

### 35.

What were the neighborhood landmarks? The ice cream shop? Drugstore? Barber shop? Grocery store? Flower shop? Shoe repair shop? What do you remember most vividly about them?

### 36.
What did your neighborhood sound like at night?

### 37.
What did your neighborhood look like first thing on a summer morning?

# ELEMENTARY SCHOOL

✍

### 1.

What was the name of your school? How big was it? Was it a public or a private school? Was it in a residential neighborhood with lots of trees around it, or on an urban street?

### 2.

What did the school building look like? One story or two stories? Brick, wood, or stone?

### 3.

Did you ride a bus to school? Do you remember anything that happened on that bus?

### 4.

Do you remember sitting at long tables, or individual desks? Do you remember sitting next to anyone in particular?

### 5.

What was the playground like at your school? Was there a swing set? Tetherball? What games did you play on the playground? Did you jump rope, play hopscotch? Did you ever play with the older kids, or did you stick with your own age group?

### 6.

Do you remember being afraid to enter first grade? What did you think when you first saw your classroom? Do you remember what decorations your teacher had up on the wall?

### 7.

Do you remember "getting" a concept? Cursive writing, maybe? Do you remember the moment when you first learned to read? Was school work hard, or easy for you?

### 8.

Did you like phys ed? Did you feel that you were good at it? Were you picked first or last for the gym team?

### 9.

Did you used to get excited thinking what you were going to wear on the first day of school? Did you ever go to a school where you had to wear a uniform?

10.

Was there a bully at school? Did he ever pick on you? How did you feel when you saw him picking on other people?

11.

Did you eat lunch at school? Did you bring it, or was there a cafeteria? What did your lunchbox look like?

12.

How did you get to school? Did you walk? Did you walk with a group of kids from the neighborhood or by yourself?

13.

Do you remember any visitors who came to visit at your school? The mayor? An actor? A cowboy star?

14.

Do you remember any field trips your class took? If you lived in the city, did you go to a farm? Did you visit a factory?

15.

What did you do in the summertime when there was no school?

16.

What was your first-grade teacher's name? What was she like? Were you in awe of her? How about your second-grade teacher? Your third-grade teacher?

17.

Did you say the "Pledge of Allegiance" to start your day? Did you say a prayer?

18.

Were you ever the new kid at school?

19.

Did you ever win any awards at school?

20.

Who was your best friend? Was it someone from the neighborhood, or did your friendships change as you met more people and had more experiences?

21.

Do you remember the names of any of your primers? Do you remember any of the drawings in them?

### 22.

Did you have a hobby during your school days? Did you ice skate or build things or perform magic? Did your schoolmates know about it or did you keep it to yourself?

### 23.

Were you in a scout troop? Who was the leader? Where did you meet?

### 24.

Who was the principal at the school? Were you ever called to the office? What was the outer office like? What was the inner office like? What was his or her desk like?

### 25.

What did you think about the older kids? Did they seem sophisticated to you? Were they able to do some activity that you just couldn't wait to do?

### 26.

What were the rules at your school? No running in the hallway? No chewing gum?

### 27.

What was your attitude about school? Were you excited about it or bored by the whole thing? Was there ever a time that you were secretly sad that it was vacation time, or did you feel the joy in days off even then?

### 28.

Do you remember kindergarten? Did you take naps there? Did you have snacks? Juice and cookies? Or milk?

### 29.

Do you remember being dropped off for your first day of kindergarten? Did your mother take you? Your father? What was it like when your parent left and you remained in the classroom?

### 30.

Did you have any friends who went with you all the way from elementary school through high school?

### 31.

Did you have an art teacher or music teacher specialist?

### 32.

What was the usual punishment at your school for pupil wrongdoings? Were kids sent into the hall to sit, were you made to sit in the corner, was there paddling? Were you ever disciplined at school? Was this embarrassing to you?

### 33.

Do you ever remember your mother coming to your school?

### 34.

Did you have class plays or room programs? Did you have big parts in them, or were you stage shy? Did you ever have to sing a solo? What costumes did you wear?

### 35.

Do you remember having to stand up in front of the class to read a paper or a story? Did you have to do multiplication tables at the blackboard?

### 36.

Can you remember a historic event that happened when you were in school? Who told you about it? Your teacher? Your mother, when you got home?

# HOLIDAYS AND CELEBRATIONS

❧

### 1.

Do you like your birthday or do you dread it? What birthday do you remember the most from your youth? What kind of parties did your parents give for you?

### 2.

Did you get a special meal for your birthday? On the actual birthday or the night before?

### 3.

Did anyone ever give you a surprise party? Were you surprised?

### 4.

Where was the Christmas tree in your house when you were growing up? Where did you hang your stockings? What did your stocking look like? Where do you put your tree and hang your stockings now?

### 5.

Did you ever spend Christmas away from home?

6.

What Christmas decorations did you put up every
year? What did you do on Christmas Eve? Or on
Hanukkah? Was Passover an important occasion in
your house? What were your Seders like?

7.

What was your Christmas dinner? Whom did you
share it with? If you celebrated Hanukkah, did that
holiday seem more spread out than you felt Christmas was? Did you ever discuss the difference in the
two holidays with your friends who celebrated
Christmas?

8.

Is there a Christmas present, a Hanukkah present,
or a birthday present that sticks out in your mind?
Who gave it to you? Was it a surprise, or something
you'd been wanting and wanting?

9.

Did you have a Sweet Sixteen party? Were you a
Bar or Bat Mitzvah? Did any birthday feel like a real
passage for you? What did you do the day you
turned twenty-one?

10.

Turned forty?

### 11.

Turned fifty?

### 12.

Have you attended a Christening, Bar Mitzvah, Baptism, or wedding of any of your grandchildren? What were your own children's ceremonies like?

### 13.

Did you ever have a shower? For a wedding or for a baby? Who was there? What presents do you remember getting?

### 14.

Do you like costume parties? What have you gone dressed as?

### 15.

What was Halloween like for you growing up? Did you play tricks on people? What costumes do you remember wearing? What kids did you go trick-or-treating with?

### 16.

What Halloween candy do you pass out?

### 17.

What other parents went with you when you took your own kids out for Halloween? Did you stay in your own neighborhood or take them to haunted houses elsewhere?

### 18.

Did you make them their costumes? What did they go out as?

### 19.

Did you and your schoolmates exchange Valentines in elementary school? Did you make them yourselves? Do you remember what any of them looked like? Did you keep them in a handmade packet?

### 20.

Did you ever get flowers for Valentine's Day? Did you ever get candy in a heart-shaped box?

### 21.

Do you send Valentines now? Do you still get them?

### 22.

Do you like to go out on New Year's Eve? What was the fanciest New Year's Eve party you ever attended?

### 23.

When you were a child, who dyed the Easter eggs in your household? Who hid the eggs? Did you get a new Easter outfit every year?

### 24.

Did you ever dress up as the Easter Bunny or Santa to surprise your children?

### 25.

When was the first Father's Day you felt like a father? The first Mother's Day you felt like a mother? What did your children do for you in celebration?

### 26.

What did you do for your parents on those days?

### 27.

As a child, where did you watch fireworks on the Fourth of July? Did you celebrate the holiday with another family?

### 28.

Did you have picnics? What did you eat? Where did you go?

### 29.

Do you celebrate the religious holidays with other members of your religious community? Does your family have a formal celebration or observance?

### 30.

Was there ever a time you went to a clergyman's home? What did it feel like there? What personal things about the clergyman did you find out from being in his home?

### 31.

Where did you go for Thanksgiving? Was there a dish your family was assigned to bring?

### 32.

Was there a centerpiece that your family used every Thanksgiving?

### 33.

Did you make birthday cakes yourself or did you buy them? What are the favorite kinds of your family members?

### 34.

What kind of birthday parties did you give for your children? Did you ever have a clown or a pony?

### 35.

What did Christmas morning feel like when you were a child? Was it hard getting to sleep the night before?

### 36.

Do you remember a holiday you had to spend alone?

### 37.

Which was the best holiday of your life? The worst?

### 38.

Do you make a lot of phone calls on holidays?

# HIGH SCHOOL

ॐ

### 1.

What was the name of your high school? What kind of neighborhood was it in? What street was it on? How many students went there? What did the hallways look and feel and sound like?

### 2.

What was your high school mascot? What were your school colors? Do you remember any of the cheers?

### 3.

Who were your friends? What did you like about them?

### 4.

What teachers do you remember? Why? Do you remember any rumors you ever heard about a teacher? Were they true?

### 5.

What was your favorite song in high school?

### 6.

What kind of extra-curricular activities did you do in high school? Were you on the school paper? A sports team? Were you a class officer? A cheerleader? Were your friends involved in the same activities as you were?

### 7.

Were you ever honored at school? Varsity letter? Homecoming court? Valedictorian? Do you remember the students who were?

### 8.

Do you remember any students whom you felt sorry for, whom other students made fun of or took advantage of?

### 9.

Were you a diligent scholar, or did you have a more casual approach?

### 10.

Did you study a foreign language? Have any phrases from that class stuck with you? Were you ever able to use that language on a vacation, or in your community?

### 11.

Did science or math come hard to you? Did art or English come easy?

### 12.

Do you remember any long papers you wrote, or any special projects?

### 13.

What did you keep in your locker? Whose locker was your locker near? Whom did you want to see in the halls? Whom did you want to avoid?

### 14.

Who did you go to your prom with? What did you wear? What was the theme? Did you dance much? Did you give, or receive, a corsage?

### 15.

Were you a rebel? Did you hide anything from your parents?

### 16.

Did you have a hobby, or did you spend your high school years mostly just hanging around with your crowd? Did you have any part-time jobs? Did you baby-sit for a family in the neighborhood?

### 17.

Were you popular? If you weren't, does that still hurt?

### 18.

Did you have a class ring? Was it a big expense for you to buy it? Did you ever trade rings with anyone? Did you go steady?

### 19.

Where did your crowd hang out? Did you go to a diner or a drugstore or a grocery or the library or a neighborhood gas station?

### 20.

What were the clothing trends when you were in high school? Did you follow those trends? What did your parents think? Did they like the way you got yourself up, or were your looks distressing to them?

### 21.

Who was your principal? Who was your gym teacher? Who was the coach of the football team?

### 22.

Was there a library at your school? Did you utilize it, or have fun with your friends there? Can you remember a particular book you checked out? Was it for your reading pleasure, or for a report you were working on?

### 23.
Was schoolwork hard or easy for you?

### 24.
Did your parents like your girlfriend or boyfriend?

### 25.
Were you happy in high school? Did you know it at the time?

### 26.
How did you get to school? Did you walk? Who did you walk with? Did you drive? Who did you drive with? Who drove?

### 27.
Were you in a clique?

### 28.
Did you ever hang out with anybody from a completely different group? Did you have any friends from different schools?

### 29.

Where did you have lunch? Did you go home, or eat in the cafeteria? Did you pack a lunch or buy it?

### 30.

Did you ever skip school? Were you ever caught? Did you ever get disciplined at school? What was your infraction? Were you really in the wrong?

### 31.

What did you do after school? Did you usually go right home? Did you often go to a friend's house? Did you work? Did you do your homework after school?

### 32.

Where did you sit to do your homework? In your room or at the kitchen table? Were your brothers and sisters with you, or did you work alone? Did you have the radio playing?

### 33.

How did you usually spend your weekends? Did your parents have you doing chores around the house? Did you spend more time at one friend's house than anyone else's? At whose house did people gather? How did their parents like having all the kids around?

34.
What did you discover about yourself in high school? Did you learn a skill that you could take out in the world with you? Were you sad when it ended, or were you ready to leave it all behind?

35.
Would you rather be in high school back when you were, or today?

36.
Have you ever attended a high school reunion? What truths did you learn about your class while you were there? What truths about your community that you might not have thought about before?

37.
Was there another student you admired more than any other? A student you wished you could have dated or been friends with?

38.
How important were your high school years in your life? Do you ever dream about those years?

### 39.

If you today could have one conversation with yourself when you were a high school student, what would you say?

### 40.

When you evaluate your life today, how much of the high school you do you see in yourself?

### 41.

What was the best night of your high school life?

# COLLEGE

### 1.

If you went to college, where did you go? Why did you choose that school? Did you have friends who went there, or was it the locale? How much was tuition? Was it difficult to afford? Did you receive financial assistance or a scholarship? A loan?

### 2.

Was your school large or small? What was it known for? Where else did you apply?

### 3.

Did you attend any kind of graduate school?

### 4.

What was your living situation? Did you live in a dorm or a room off campus? Who was your roommate? Did you get along? How did you decorate your place? Were you comfortable there?

### 5.

What was your major? Why did you pick it? Were you ever able to use anything you learned in college in real life?

### 6.

Did you join a sorority or fraternity? What was rush week like? Were you frightened that you would not get chosen, or were you pretty confident that you would be recognized?

### 7.

What was the symbol, the saying, the pin, the handshake of your fraternal organization?

### 8.

Who was your big brother or big sister?

### 9.

Have you ever been to a college reunion? Was it fun, or sort of sad? Did you see anyone there whom you were surprised and happy to see?

### 10.

When you first got to college, were you thrilled to be away from home? If you were homesick, what did you do about it? Write letters? Cry? Confide in someone? Or try to hide your feelings? If you were thrilled to be at college, were you quick at making friends? Who was your first friend there? Did you remain close through the years?

### 11.

Were you on any sports teams? If not, did you follow them? What was the mascot? The school colors? Were any of your teams champions or near-champs?

### 12.

Were there "big weekends" at your college? Did you attend these functions? Who was your date? Were you ever on a committee to put on one of these events? Was there a lot of drinking going on? How did people "party" in those days?

### 13.

Was there any professor who made a special impression on you? Good or bad? What subject did he or she teach? Were you able to take more than one class from this person? Did he or she ever make a comment about your work that stuck in your memory?

### 14.

Why was it important for you to go to college? Was it an expected step in your community, or were you the first in your family to go for a degree? What motivated you most? Love of learning, or just getting through?

### 15.

Were you able to get home for the holidays? How did you get there? By train? By bus? How long did the trip take? Did you meet anyone you remember on one of these trips? Did anything memorable happen?

### 16.

Did you remain friendly with anyone you met at college? Did you visit each other over the years? Did you keep in touch by letter?

### 17.

Did you change much at college? Did your parents notice? Did your friends back home notice? Did they mention it to you?

### 18.

Did you have a raccoon coat? Did your college chums go in for any fads or antics?

### 19.

Were you involved in campus politics? Was this hard to fit in with your studies?

### 20.

Was your class work difficult or easy for you? What were your study habits? Did you pull all-nighters? Did you cram with friends, or work alone?

### 21.

Did you have a part-time job while you were in school?

### 22.

What did you notice about students from other parts of the country? Accents? Different taste in clothing?

### 23.

Was there one class that particularly inspired you? Was there one that felt just impossible?

### 24.

What degree did you get? Did you attend graduation?

### 25.

Who were some famous graduates from your school? Anyone you could tell would be a big success even then?

### 26.

Did you change colleges partway through? Why?

### 27.

Did you have your own phone or did you have to speak in a hallway? Were phone calls commonplace then, or was communication with your family mainly through the mail?

### 28.

Did you win any accolades at college? Phi Beta Kappa? Valedictorian? *Magna cum laude?*

### 29.

Did any famous performers or lecturers appear at your college?

### 30.

Do you think you made the most of your college years, or would it have been more advantageous for you to have gone to school later on?

### 31.

Which do you have fonder memories of—college or high school?

### 32.

Did college ever start to feel like home to you? Or was it always just a stopping-off place?

### 33.

Did your friends back home who didn't go to college treat you differently when you came home for Thanksgiving, Christmas, or the summer? How did it make you feel?

### 34.

Were you the same person when you got out of college as when you entered as a freshman?

# MILITARY CAREER

### 1.

Name, rank, and serial number?

### 2.

Were you drafted or did you enlist? What was the first you saw of the service—the enlistment center? What did you see there that made you want to sign up? What was it like at the draft board?

### 3.

What was the name of your company? Did it have a nickname? Did it have a mascot?

### 4.

Where were you stationed? Describe what it was like.

### 5.

How quickly did you move up through the ranks? Who was the first officer you admired?

### 6.

Did you win any medals or citations? What for? Where do you keep that medal now—is it prominently displayed in your house, or is it stashed away in a drawer? Who handed it to you? Was there a ceremony?

### 7.

What USO entertainers did you see perform? Which of your buddies did you sit with when you saw the program?

### 8.

What songs do you remember hearing during the war? Which song most says "war years" to you?

### 9.

What did your uniform look like? How did you feel you looked in it? Do you still have any of it in a closet somewhere?

### 10.

What supplies and weaponry were you issued? How long did it take you to learn to use your weapon? What was the situation on the practice range? Was it far from your quarters? Were you a pretty good shot?

### 11.

Where did you go through basic training? Were you with any of your hometown buddies? How tough was it? Which part did you excel in; in which part did you lag behind? Who was the officer in charge?

### 12.

Describe your barracks—from basic training on up. Who were your bunk mates? Were you close with any of them?

### 13.

Was military food as bad as it's cracked up to be, or was it okay? What were some of your typical meals?

### 14.

What were your duties and assignments, in camp and on the field? Were you in the motor pool? Did you work KP?

### 15.

Who were your best buddies? Are you still in touch with any of them?

### 16.

Who did you write letters to? Who did you get letters from? What time did the mail come every day? What was that like?

### 17.

What commander did you get along the worst with? Was there one you were friendly with?

### 18.

When did you first see combat? Did it take you by surprise, or did you know it was coming?

### 19.

When did you first see death? Did you lose any of your good friends?

### 20.

Where did you go for R and R? Was it a debauched time, or was it fairly good, clean fun? What did you see on one of these trips that you had never seen before?

### 21.

Who took you to the train when you were to report for duty? Was it a teary farewell?

### 22.

What was the date of your swearing in? What was the date of your discharge?

### 23.

What was your theater of operation? What did you learn about the culture of that country? How did the citizenry differ from the citizenry of your country?

### 24.

Where did you go on maneuvers? Were they a reasonable facsimile of real warfare?

### 25.

When you get together with buddies to tell war stories, what stories do you tell?

### 26.

What was the biggest act of courage you saw? By an ally? By an enemy?

### 27.

When you think of your years in the service, what landscape describes it best? Flat, low ground? Mountains? A long, steep highway?

### 28.

Do you remember your homecoming? Was the final leg of your homecoming by train? Who was there at the station to meet you?

### 29.

Do you remember your homecoming with your parents? What did you have to eat for your first meal back home?

### 30.

Was there a love waiting for you when you came back home, or were you unattached? Did the war make you ready to settle down, or did you come home in a more crazy, celebratory mood?

### 31.

Did you ever consider re-upping? What were your thoughts about enlisting again?

### 32.

Were there photos of pinup girls on the walls of your barracks? Who were they?

### 33.

Everyone knows that war itself is bad, but when you look back on your own years in the service, are your personal memories predominantly good or bad ones?

### 34.

How difficult was the transition from the military back to civilian life? Was the famous movie *The Best Years of Our Lives* a pretty accurate representation of those times?

### 35.

Are you a member of a veterans' organization? Are you active in it? What does it add to your life?

# HOMEFRONT

### 1.

Were you married to a serviceman or did you have a sweetheart in the service?

### 2.

Where were you when he got his orders? How did he break the news to you? How did you react outwardly? Inwardly? Was a separation like that a common occurrence for your friends during the war years?

### 3.

Did you stay near a stateside base with him? Were you friendly with the other wives? Who were your friends when your mate was in the service? Did you and your friends spend Saturday nights together?

### 4.

Where did you live? Did you go back and stay with your parents? Did you keep up the household by yourself?

### 5.

Did you work? What job did you do? Were many of the people in the workplace women with men overseas?

### 6.

Were your brothers in the service? Was your father a military man?

### 7.

Were your children born at the time? Were they old enough to miss their daddy?

### 8.

How often did you write? Every day? Where were you when you wrote your letters? At the desk in the living room? At the kitchen table? Lying on your bed?

### 9.

What time did your mail come? How often did you receive a letter from your sweetheart? Do you remember anything particular that one of those letters said?

### 10.

Did you ever hear news of the war on the radio that affected your loved one directly? Did you find you were frightened every time the news came on? When did you usually listen? After dinner? In the morning? In which room of the house was the radio where you usually listened to the news?

### 11.

Did you ever do any volunteer work for the war effort? Did you roll bandages for the Red Cross?

### 12.

When did you hear that your sweetheart was coming home? Where were you when you got the news? Who told you?

### 13.

How long was it between hearing the news and when he got home? Did the time go by quickly or slowly?

### 14.

What changes were there in everyday life between wartime and peacetime? Was gas rationing difficult for you? Did you save aluminum foil? Did you shop differently? What were your town's air-raid drills like? Was there a certain sadness and fear that you felt in the streets?

15.

Did any of your friends lose husbands in the war?

16.

Do you still have the letters that he sent you?
When was the last time you read one of them?

17.

Did you know men who stayed in town because
they couldn't join the military for one reason or
another?

18.

What kinds of clothes were in style at the time?
What outfit do you remember? What outfits do you
remember your friends wearing?

19.

What newspapers did you read at the time? Do you
remember any certain headline?

20.

Did you send any packages overseas? Did your
sweetheart bring you a souvenir from his travels?

### 21.

Did you keep a picture of him up in the house? Where? On the living room end table? On your nightstand?

### 22.

What pictures did you send him of yourself?

### 23.

What did you learn to do yourself during the war years that you never expected you'd have to do? What made you the proudest? What gave you the most moments of worry?

### 24.

How did you sign your letters? Do you remember?

### 25.

Did you write to any servicemen other than your sweetheart?

### 26.

What were your feelings about America's position in the war?

### 27.

Did your feelings about war then color your feelings about war now?

### 28.

Did you have any frightening dreams when your sweetheart was away?

### 29.

Did you ever have to visit a parent whose son was killed in the war?

### 30.

Was anyone you ever knew missing in action?

### 31.

Were your feelings about the war when it was going on different from your feelings about the war now, looking back?

### 32.

What was it like in your city on the day the war ended?

# ENTERTAINMENT

ॐ

### 1.

What was your favorite radio show growing up? What did your radio look like? What room was it in? Did your family sit around and listen to programs together? What time, what day or night were they on? Did you sit on the davenport, lie on the floor, or sit around the kitchen table when you listened?

### 2.

Did you ever go to see a favorite performer in concert when you were young? Frank Sinatra? Tommy Dorsey?

### 3.

What were the plot lines of some of the most popular radio shows of the day? Do you remember which companies sponsored which shows? Even though you couldn't see the actors, did you have pictures of what they looked like in your mind? Were you surprised when you found out what certain actors actually did look like?

4.

What radio stations do you listen to now? What are their slogans? Do you ever tune in talk radio? Have you ever called a talk-radio host and had your voice go on the air?

5.

Have your tastes in entertainment been fairly mainstream, or have you gone for more unusual music or cinema? Do you like jazz or foreign films? Do you go to poetry readings?

6.

What is your preference in music? Are you a country fan, rhythm-and-blues fan, or do you listen to classical music exclusively?

7.

When did you get your first TV? Did you buy it so your family could view a special show or event? What room did you put it in? How much did it cost? Who actually carried it into your house? Was your family one of the first in your neighborhood to have a TV?

8.

Have you bought any new home entertainment gadgets lately? Do you own a VCR? A CD player?

A Walkman? How long did it take you to get used to using them?

### 9.

Are you a theatergoer? Do you go in your hometown or only when you visit a big city?

### 10.

What movie affected you most in your life? Do you remember the way the movie looked mostly, or was it the story line? Who were the stars? Was there music in the movie that you remember?

### 11.

What movies have you wanted to see more than once?

### 12.

What was the last movie you saw? What was the first movie you saw?

### 13.

Did you ever own any records of Broadway musicals? Which ones? Where did you keep your record albums? In a bookshelf? Under the hi fi? Did you have many? Which ones did your kids like, too?

### 14.

How much TV do you watch? Do you watch more now than you used to? What show have you continued to enjoy through the years? Are any of your favorites in reruns now? Which TV shows do you wish they'd bring back?

### 15.

Which Ed Sullivan shows do you remember most? Fred Allen shows? Jack Benny shows?

### 16.

Which TV shows are really dumb, but you like anyway?

### 17.

Which comedian makes you laugh the hardest? Do you like them squeaky-clean or do you go in for the racier type? Did you ever buy comedy albums? *The Button-Down Mind of Bob Newhart,* or something like that? Did you listen in a family group?

### 18.

Have you ever been a contestant on a game show or in the studio audience of a talk show?

### 19.

Do you enjoy watching ballet or other dance?

20.

Have you ever wanted to be an entertainer? Have you ever appeared in local theater or in a civic organization's show?

21.

Do you attend sporting events, or any events in an outdoor arena in your town? Rodeo? Car races? Football games?

22.

Did your kids ever like an entertainer whom you hated? Like Elvis? How did you feel about the Beatles? Did you swoon over any of the crooners?

23.

How important is reading to you? Do you have an author whom you follow? Have you ever been a member of a reading club? How about a book mail-order club? Do you usually go for the selection of the month?

24.

Do you and your spouse enjoy the same entertainers and types of entertainment? Or does each of you have a different set of friends with whom you attend performances?

### 25.

Do you follow current music, or do you prefer the old?

### 26.

Do you go to matinees? Do you use a senior citizen's discount?

### 27.

What is your favorite Walt Disney film?

### 28.

Do you enjoy looking at paintings? Have you sought out gallery-going in your life?

### 29.

Do you ever watch soap operas?

### 30.

Who is your favorite talk-show host? What was the most fascinating program he or she had on? What is it about the host you like? Intelligence? Warmth? Empathy? Humor? Would you be nervous if you were somehow invited to be a guest on the program?

### 31.

Where were you during "Howdy Doody Time"? Were you in the kitchen fixing dinner? Were you in the car coming home? Were you lying on the floor in front of the set?

### 32.

Did you ever go to a 3-D movie? Who did you go with? What did you see? Did you think it worked?

### 33.

What TV performers have you seen come and go? Johnny Carson? Ernie Kovacs? Red Skelton? Do you miss their shows, or are the newer ones fine with you?

### 34.

What poetry do you find accessible? What lines from poems stick in your mind?

# CAREERS

### 1.

What was your first job? Your first real job? Did you start out in an after-school job that had any relation to what you ended up doing? Were you as nervous on the first day of your first real job as your were on the first day of your after-school job?

### 2.

Has anyone helped you up the ladder, even with the first job? Was it easy for you to ask for or accept this help?

### 3.

Are you union or management?

### 4.

Do you feel as if you were in the right business for you? What would have been your dream career?

### 5.

Were you ever the boss? Would you have wanted to be?

6.

Did you ever run your own business? How did it start?

7.

What was a "power lunch" in your day? What kind of meal was it—three martinis or the blue-plate special?

8.

Were you friendly with your coworkers? Is there one you particularly remember? Did you ever socialize in their homes, or did you sit at a table with them at the company picnic? Did you call them at night or on the weekends just to talk?

9.

Did you have a secretary? Were you very dependent on her? Did she keep pictures of her family on her desk?

10.

What was your boss like? Was he or she a frightening person or a benevolent figure? Do you remember sitting in your boss's office? Do you remember what it looked like? What your boss wore? How your boss addressed you and how you addressed your boss?

### 11.

Do you think your workplace was a friendly place for employees? What was the overriding attitude in the place? Did management mix with the rank-and-file workers? Was there a lunchroom in the workplace? Did both management and nonmanagement eat there?

### 12.

How did you feel on Mondays? How did you feel on Fridays? Were you dead tired at the end of the day? Mentally or physically? Or spiritually? Or did you often not want the day to end?

### 13.

Did you have a mentor? Were you a mentor? When did you realize that there was someone looking up to you as a professional person in your chosen career?

### 14.

Did you look forward to retirement? Did they throw a party for you at work? Did they give you a gift? What was it? Was that embarrassing to you? Is there anyone still there whom you miss? Are you tempted to call or visit your office? Did you ever give in to the temptation?

### 15.

Did you ever ride through rocky times at your workplace? Was your company sold or taken over?

### 16.

Did you feel that you had a career, or just a job?

### 17.

Did you ride mass transit to work? Did you see the same people every day? Did you speak with them, or ride in silence?

### 18.

Was there a place you went to lunch a lot at work? Was it close by? Was there one person you went to lunch with more than others? Did you often go alone?

### 19.

Did you ever eat at your desk? Did many people?

### 20.

Did you ever socialize with your boss? Did he take you out for lunch or drinks? How did that make you feel? Were you deferential to him or did you hold your ground?

### 21.

Would you call yourself ambitious?

### 22.

What about you led to the career choices you made? Special interests, or were your decisions purely economic? Or did the choice just kind of happen?

### 23.

Was your profession a respected one in your community?

### 24.

Do you think you were paid fairly at jobs throughout your life?

### 25.

Did you wake up to an alarm, a clock-radio, or the sun streaming through the window? What time did you get up? What time did you go to bed on a weeknight? Did you sleep late on the weekends?

### 26.

Was there a frequent Friday night watering hole?

## 27.

Did you ever work unusual hours? Graveyard or swing shift?

## 28.

Were you ever fired or laid off? How did you cope with that? Did you ever have to go on unemployment?

## 29.

What bank was your check drawn on? When did you get paid? Every other Friday? Once a month?

## 30.

Were you promoted? Did it come unexpectedly, or did you let it be known you wanted the job? Who told you? How did you feel and react when you heard the good news?

## 31.

Were you ever passed over for a position you thought you deserved? Who got it? Were you able to work well with this person after that? Do you remember the first meeting you had to have with him or her? How did you do?

### 32.

Did you ever have to deal with a strike at your place of business? Did you walk the picket line? Did you have to cross it? How did that affect things around the job?

### 33.

Did you define yourself by your job? Were you proud when people asked you what you did, or would you rather have been able to say something else?

### 34.

Is there a business person you particularly admire? Why?

# ROMANCE AND RELATIONSHIPS

1.

Do you remember your first kiss?

2.

What kind of dating did you do in high school?
What is your favorite kind of date, even now?

3.

Were you always attracted to the same type of person? Did you like the strong silent type? The bouncy blonde?

4.

Who was your first love? Did you think it was going to last? Who broke whose heart?

5.

Did you know, on the first day you met your spouse, that this would be your life's partner? How did you know? Did he or she know it, too?

### 6.

Describe your wedding. Your outfit. Your spouse's. Your mom's. Your dad's. The bridal party. The church or hall. The reception. The food.

### 7.

Was there anything unusual in your wedding vows? Were your knees knocking? Who performed the ceremony?

### 8.

What do you like best about your spouse? A physical attribute? A way of being or seeing? His laugh, perhaps? Or her smile?

### 9.

What were the hardest times in your marriage? Was there ever a time when you felt it might really be over?

### 10.

Can you name the china patterns, silver patterns, crystal patterns that you picked to be given to you as wedding gifts?

### 11.

Who were the big crushes in your life? What movie star did you have a crush on? What real person?

12.

What song do you consider the most romantic?

13.

What term of endearment do you use for your spouse?

14.

Did you date much before you settled down? What was your last relationship like—the one before you married your spouse? Were you unhappy when it ended? What did you learn in that relationship that helped you decide to marry the person whom you married?

15.

Everybody has bad habits. What drives you craziest about your spouse?

16.

What qualities would you choose in a mate now, if you had it to do all over again?

17.

Did you ever have an unrequited love?

### 18.

What anniversary gift do you remember giving?
What anniversary gift do you remember getting?

### 19.

Would you consider yourself a romantic? In words
or deeds? Are you the flowers-and-candy type, or
do you depend more on steadfast trustworthiness,
doing what you said you were going to do? Do you
wish your spouse had been more romantic?

### 20.

What is your favorite picture of you two together?
A wedding picture? An anniversary picture? What
photo do you have that shows the true feelings between you two?

### 21.

Did you ever go steady?

### 22.

Did you have an engagement ring? What does your
wedding ring look like? Would you ever give it up
for a bigger, shinier one? Do you both wear rings?
Are they inscribed inside?

### 23.

What did he say when he asked you to marry him? What did she answer? Where were you? Did he go to talk to your father? How was it meeting his parents?

### 24.

Name your boyfriends or girlfriends through the years.

### 25.

How did you get along with your in-laws? What did your parents have to say about your intended?

### 26.

Who is the most romantic couple you know, either real or in the movies?

### 27.

What physical feelings do you equate with feelings of love?

### 28.

Where did you go on your honeymoon? Did you ever take a second honeymoon?

### 29.

Talk about your first apartment together. Your first house. Were they places you loved, or were they just making-do?

### 30.

Looking back now, did you get married at the right time, or should you have waited longer—or done it earlier?

### 31.

In your years of marriage, what have you learned about your spouse that you didn't know on your wedding day?

# PARENTHOOD

## 1.

Do you remember telling your husband that you were pregnant? Was it a surprise, or a long-planned-for event? Do you remember telling your parents?

## 2.

What did your maternity clothes look like? Did you share with your friends? Did you suffer from morning sickness or have other problems?

## 3.

Why did you name your children what you named them?

## 4.

Which hospital did you deliver in? Do you remember the ride there? Do you remember the ride home?

## 5.

How much weight did you gain each time? Was it difficult getting back in shape?

### 6.

Who did you call first to say "It's a boy!" or "It's a girl!"? Can you remember what you said when the doctor or nurse first handed you your baby? Can you remember what your spouse said?

### 7.

Did you send birth announcements when your babies were born? Did you have help in the house? A nurse or nanny?

### 8.

Did you have a separate nursery all fixed up? How was it papered and painted? What did the crib look like? Did you hang a mobile over it?

### 9.

What pet name did you use for your children when they were babies? Did you keep using them, even when the children grew older?

### 10.

Did any of your kids have an imaginary friend growing up? Were they afraid of the boogeyman or the monster under the bed?

### 11.

What was your children's favorite bedtime story or poem?

### 12.

Were you involved in many carpools? Did you teach your child to drive?

### 13.

How did you decide which school to send your children to? Did they go to the neighborhood school, or did you send them to private or parochial school? Why?

### 14.

Did you use any books when you were raising your children? Dr. Spock? *Where Did You Go? Out. What Did You Do? Nothing?* Did they help?

### 15.

Did your babies have hair when they were born?

### 16.

Did you send your kids to camp? Did you sew name tags on their clothes? Was it difficult for you to have them gone, or did you find it a welcome break? Did you attend parents' weekends? Did you become friendly with any of the other parents there?

### 17.

Did you buy your children a set of encyclopedias? What kind? Where did you keep them? Did they use them very much?

### 18.

What did you do to punish your kids? Was this hard for you to do? Which of your children needed the most discipline? Why, do you think?

### 19.

What did your kids call you? The basic "Mommy" and "Daddy" or something more unusual?

### 20.

Did your kids play in the backyards in the neighborhood, or did you take them to a park?

### 21.

Did you have a rocking chair for your babies? Where was it? Downstairs, or in the nursery?

22.

Did they play in a playpen? What toys did you keep in there? What was the highchair like?

23.

Did you send them to religious school?

24.

Were you involved in the PTA or as a room parent at school? Did a teacher ever call you in to discuss a problem, or to tell you something about your child that made you very proud?

25.

What TV shows do you remember your kids watching? Did you watch any of these programs with them? Did you allow them to eat in front of the TV?

26.

Who was your children's pediatrician? Did you ever have to take them to the emergency room?

27.

Whom did you hire to baby-sit? What was the going rate?

### 28.

Were the teenage years rugged for you and your kids?

### 29.

How did you cope with taking them to college?

### 30.

What was the scariest moment in parenting? The toughest? The moment that made you most proud?

### 31.

Did your children ever have a slumber party at your house? Did they like to go to them?

### 32.

Can you remember one memorable thing that each one of your children said, something that surprised you or amused you or impressed you at the time and still sticks in your mind?

### 33.

What was the best part of being a parent? The worst?

### 34.

What was the best trip you ever took with your children? What made it so good?

### 35.

What one thing would you do differently if you could live your parenting years over?

### 36.

What was the transition like when you went from being someone's child to being someone's parent? How long did it take you to really get used to the idea?

# THE HOUSE YOU RAISED YOUR FAMILY IN

ও

### 1.

Was the house you raised your family in big enough for all of you? Did your kids share a room? Did you ever move? Was that particularly hard on anyone?

### 2.

What was your address? What was your phone number?

### 3.

Was your house a one-story, two-story? Stone, wood, or brick? Did you have a garage? A black-top driveway? What was the floor plan? Did you use the back door as much as you used the front?

### 4.

Can you envision each room, and certain things that went on there? Can you remember certain conversations that took place in those rooms?

### 5.

What was the view out your front window?

6.

Was your neighborhood one of single-family homes, apartment buildings, or was it widely spaced and rural? Were you friendly with your neighbors? Was everyone in and out of one another's homes?

7.

Did you eat at the kitchen table, or in the dining room? What did your tables and chairs look like? Who sat where?

8.

What did you hang on your refrigerator door?

9.

How many bathrooms did you have? How many baths? How many showers? Was there a long line-up in the morning? Who bathed in the evening, who preferred a shower?

10.

Why did you originally move to the town where you lived? How did you pick the neighborhood? Did you choose it for the schools, for the quiet, for the proximity to your workplace?

### 11.

What kind of stove did you have? Gas or electric? Did you have linoleum on the kitchen floor? What was the pattern? What did your cookie jars and canisters look like?

### 12.

Where did you keep the goodies? In a special drawer or cupboard? Where did you keep your paper grocery bags? Where did you keep your onions and potatoes?

### 13.

Where did you keep your ironing board? Where did you do your wash?

### 14.

Did anyone live with you other than family members? Were you friendly with them, or was it a tenant-renter relationship?

### 15.

What room did your family relax in together? Where did you go to get away from one another? Did the kids hang out in their rooms?

### 16.

Did they keep their rooms messy? Did that bother you? Did you insist that they made their beds every day?

### 17.

Where did your kids throw their books when they got home from school? Where did they do their homework? Were they good about it, or did you have to prod? Did you have to help them with big projects?

### 18.

What were the rules of the house? No phone calls after ten P.M.? Last one in, lock the door?

### 19.

Which lights did you leave on all night? What did those night lamps look like?

### 20.

Where did you throw your mail?

### 21.

Did you ever undertake a big remodeling job? Did you wallpaper and paint? Did you buy new carpeting? Did you pave the driveway? Were you ever tempted to build a pool?

### 22.

Where were your telephones?

### 23.

Did you have a basement? What was down there? Did you have an attic? What was up there?

### 24.

Was your house a gathering place for your friends or for your children's friends? Did they eat you out of house and home? What snacks did you keep on hand to offer them to eat or drink?

### 25.

Did you have swing sets, a basketball hoop, a sandbox?

### 26.

Did you have lilac trees and forsythia bushes? Did spring smell like spring where you lived?

### 27.

Can you feel your doorknob in your hand when you think about it now? Can you feel the bannister in your hand? Can you visualize the kitchen cupboards?

### 28.

Did you have to walk up steps to get to your front door? What was on the corner of your street when you rounded it to come home?

### 29.

Did your house have awnings or shutters? What color was the house painted? What color was the trim?

### 30.

Did your family sit outside much in the summer? On a patio or a front stoop? Did you have a screened-in porch? A front porch? Did you ever eat meals out there?

### 31.

Where did everybody hang their overcoats?

### 32.

Did you ever have the house to yourself? Did you enjoy it? Or did it feel lonely and empty? Were there times when you felt confined by the house? Was there a place in the house you could go for privacy?

### 33.

When your children moved out, did the house feel like a different place? Did you like it as much?

### 34.

What was your favorite part of the house? Why?

### 35.

What was it like the day you moved in? What was it like the day you moved out?

### 36.

If you were starting over and had to raise your family all over again, is that house the house you'd choose to do it in?

### 37.

Do you still live in the house? If not, how does it make you feel when you think of another family living there? Have you ever gone back to visit the house? Was it a good experience, or did you regret going?

# $\mathcal{F}$AVORITES

### 1.

What's your favorite candy bar? Where do you usually buy it? At the drugstore or the grocery store? How much does it cost now? How much did it cost when you were growing up? Was there a particular task you ever did that you would reward yourself for doing by buying yourself a candy?

### 2.

What's your favorite kind of cake? Does it come from a restaurant or does someone you know bake it? Do you ask for a rose on your piece of birthday cake?

### 3.

What about ice cream? What kind do you like? Do you get it at an ice cream parlor or in the freezer section of a store? Did your summers include walking to get ice cream cones? Who did you usually go with? Your brother or sister? Your best friend? Which is for you, sugar or cake cones?

### 4.

What's your favorite saying? What does it mean to you? Why is it important to you? Can you remember where you first heard it?

### 5.

What is your favorite perfume or cologne? Do you remember seeing an ad about it that intrigued you, or did you smell it on someone else and just have to have it? Did you ever receive your perfume as a surprise, or was it such a well-known fact about you that you got it for a present more often than not?

### 6.

What is your favorite book? Have you read it more than once? Do you own a copy, or take it out of the library? Have you ever suggested it to anyone as a particularly good read? Have they liked it as well as you did? Have they understood?

### 7.

What is your favorite song? When was the first time you heard it? Did you own a copy, or did you wait to hear it on the radio? Have you ever had a chance to use the song in a personal ceremony: your wedding, a big anniversary party, a birthday celebration?

### 8.

What's your favorite movie? How old were you when you saw it? At what theater? Who did you go with? Did you want to see the stars of that movie in other movies?

### 9.

What's your drink? At what age did you start drinking? Did you take that first drink at a party, or in a drinking establishment? Do you have a regular bar or bartender? Have you ever had one too many?

### 10.

What's your favorite season? What do you like most/least about summer? About fall? What special foods do you eat in the summer? How do you winterize your home? Do you garden in spring?

### 11.

Who is your sports team? Baseball? Basketball? Football? Pro? College? Do you attend games or watch on TV? Would you say you are a super fan, or a fair-weather friend? Have you ever met the coach? Do you respect him?

### 12.

Did you ever have a sports figure who was particularly meaningful to you? Did you ever get his or her autograph?

### 13.

Do you have a favorite Broadway or movie musical? Did you ever actually see it on stage? Or do you just like the music?

### 14.

Who is your favorite author or literary figure? Do you make it a point to try to read everything he or she writes?

### 15.

Whose politics have you admired most? What president would you have most enjoyed voting for? Abraham Lincoln? Andrew Jackson? Who was the best president of your lifetime?

### 16.

Who is your favorite artist? Have you ever seen his or her work "in person," or only in books? Do you know much about the artist's personal life? Do you identify with the artist's life in any way?

### 17.

Who is your favorite male movie star? Female movie star? Have you ever written a fan letter?

### 18.

How about television stars?

### 19.

Different times of life are satisfying for different reasons; which has been the most satisfying for you? Why? The three-kids-and-the-station-wagon stage? When you became the boss? When you were pursuing your higher education?

### 20.

The least satisfying?

### 21.

Who is your best friend?

### 22.

What is your favorite holiday? Where do you celebrate it? Where did you celebrate it when you were growing up?

### 23.

Do you have a favorite retreat or place of respite where you go to bring you silence and solace?

What situation brought you to appreciate such a place? Did you have a secret hideout as a youth?

### 24.

What is your favorite cartoon character or comic strip? Do you ever cut out panels of these and post them on your refrigerator? Which comics do you remember reading when you were growing up?

### 25.

What is your favorite restaurant? What special dish do you like to eat there? Do you know the maitre d' or hostess? Are you friendly with the waitresses or waiters? Do you like to sit at the same table every time?

### 26.

Is there a toast you use time and time again? Do you always toast your companions? Can you remember a time you were toasted that touched you particularly?

### 27.

What is your favorite flower? Do you grow it in your garden or buy it at a florist or nursery? Did you have a sweetheart who often gave flowers to you? On holidays or as a surprise? Can you remember the first bouquet you ever received?

### 28.

What is your favorite color? Do you have clothing in this color or have you painted the walls of your house this color? Have you bought a car in this color?

### 29.

What is your favorite game show or talk show? Which ones did you like that aren't broadcast any longer?

### 30.

What modern conveniences are your favorites? The portable phone? The remote control?

### 31.

Is there an old item of clothing that you can't make yourself throw away?

### 32.

What is your favorite time of day? Do you have a certain ritual you do at sunset every day, or first thing in the morning?

### 33.

What was the best day of your life?

# FOOD

### 1.

How do you like your eggs? Where do you usually get them, in a coffee shop or at home? Who makes them at your house? You or your spouse? What kind of omelette do you order?

### 2.

What is your favorite restaurant meal?

### 3.

What recipe are you famous for? For a small group? For a large group? What dish do you usually bring to a potluck or picnic?

### 4.

What is your McDonald's order? Do you get the same thing every time? Do you ever get a McDonald's dessert? What kind of milkshake do you order?

### 5.

How do you take your coffee? Do you have a favorite coffee mug? Where do you drink it in the morning? Do you ever drink it at night?

### 6.

What would be your last supper?

### 7.

What is your favorite Campbell's soup?

### 8.

Do you follow any rules of nutrition? Are you a vegetarian? Do you stay away from white sugar? Do you keep Kosher? Eat fish on Friday? Avoid cholesterol?

### 9.

Have you ever had breakfast brought to you in bed?

### 10.

What kind of toast do you eat? Rye? Wheat? Do you take jam or jelly on it? What flavor?

### 11.

What kind of salad dressing do you usually choose? Do you prefer iceberg or dark-green lettuce?

### 12.

Have you ever been on a diet? A faddish diet that "everyone" was on? What diet worked the best for you? How much do you remember losing?

### 13.

Are you brand-loyal? What are some of the brands you've stuck with all your life? How do you feel about generic goods? Do you buy store-brand food? Drugs? Vitamins? Cleaning goods?

### 14.

What's the water like in your town? Drinkable? Do you have to get the bottled kind? Or do you get the bottled kind by choice?

### 15.

What microwave food do you find tasty? How often do you eat it?

### 16.

What are your personal staples? What stuff do you keep around the house all the time?

### 17.

What is your perfect breakfast? What is your usual breakfast?

18.

What is your perfect lunch? What is your usual lunch?

19.

What is your perfect dinner? What is your usual dinner?

20.

What is your favorite snack?

21.

What cookbook do you use most? What one do you remember your mother using?

22.

What is your favorite fruit? Your favorite vegetable? Which ones do you think of when you think of the different seasons? Did you shop for produce at a produce stand? What was the best thing you were able to buy fresh?

23.

Do you eat seafood? Have you ever eaten it at the shore?

### 24.

Are you allergic to any foods? Is there anything that you cannot stand and will not eat?

### 25.

What is your weakness? Sweets?

### 26.

How do you keep from crying when you cut onions?

### 27.

What do you like on your pizza? What do you order in a Chinese restaurant? How do you like your steak cooked? Where were the best places you've ever had these foods?

### 28.

What do you remember as your mother's specialty item? Your grandmothers'?

### 29.

Do you enjoy a good outdoor barbecue?

### 30.

What tastes do you still crave from your youth? Philly cheese steaks? Egg creams? Onion rings from a little diner in your town? Something your mother made?

### 31.

What do you like to drink with your meals? Iced tea? Milk? A milkshake?

### 32.

What is your corn-on-the-cob etiquette? Do you use corn holders? Do you have special corn-on-the-cob plates? Do you eat around the ear, or left to right, typewriter-style?

### 33.

Do you eat better or worse now than when you were a child?

### 34.

Did you ever have a memorable meal on a train?

### 35.

Do you feel full more easily than you did when you were younger? Do you wish you didn't?

### 36.

What do you remember about your first trips to a grocery store? To a supermarket?

### 37.

Do you think fast food was a good development or a bad one?

### 38.

What was the most delicious meal you've ever had?

### 39.

What is your earliest memory of a restaurant meal?

### 40.

When you are by yourself in a hotel, do you prefer ordering room service to sitting by yourself in the hotel restaurant?

### 41.

Was eating a meal more fun before everyone knew how bad certain foods are for us?

### 42.

What was it like eating at a soda fountain when you were young?

# MOMENTS FROM YOUR ADULT LIFE

∽

### 1.

Did you and your spouse often go dancing? Where? In a big dance pavilion? Did you get excited when you pulled into the parking lot?

### 2.

What bands did you dance to? Any of the famous Big Bands? What songs do you remember them playing? Did you prefer dancing to fast songs, or slow songs? Why?

### 3.

Which dances did you do? Where did you learn to do these dances?

### 4.

When you and your friends got together socially, what did you do? Cards? Charades? Conversation? Small talk? Whose house did you go to most often, or did you trade off?

#### 5.

What rooms do you remember you and your friends gathering in? Was the TV on? Were there children playing around you?

#### 6.

Do you remember when your friends had babies? Did their babies cry more or less than yours did? Did the babies play together? When they got older and went to school, did they remain friends?

#### 7.

How did you meet the friend you're most comfortable with now? How did you meet the couple you're most comfortable with now?

#### 8.

What kind of movies do you find yourself drawn to? Do you like adventure or romance? Epic or light comedy? Do you like discussing a movie after you've seen it, or do you just tend to enjoy it while it's going on, and keep the experience to yourself? Do you go to movies now as much as you used to? Do you rent videocassettes? How do you choose which ones to rent?

### 9.

What kind of books do you enjoy reading? Novels? Biographies? Do you buy them new or borrow them from the library? Do you have a "library" in your house?

### 10.

What is the last book you read? Why did you choose that one? Where were you sitting when you read it?

### 11.

Are you friendly with your neighbors? Do you sit down together of an evening on the back porch or the patio? Or are you merely cordial with them, nodding acquaintances? Do you look out for one another's homes when one of you goes away?

### 12.

Have you ever had a neighbor whom you've loved and lost? Were you close with a family that later moved away?

### 13.

Are you now, or have you ever been, a member of any club, social group, or organization?

### 14.

Have you spent time doing charitable work? Did you put in legwork, hours on the phone, or office volunteer work? Why was the charity you picked important to you? Did you meet people working there whom you would not have met in your everyday life?

### 15.

Is there anything that you need that you do not have?

### 16.

Do you take a little respite for yourself every day? A drink before dinner? A walk after? A morning constitutional? A morning spa?

### 17.

Do you have planned recreation? A Wednesday night bowling league? A Thursday morning tennis game? Or do you take exercise catch-as-catch-can?

### 18.

Do you do any weekly social activity: bridge at your sister and brother-in-law's? Poker at the club? What other things do you look forward to doing?

19.

Have you ever had surgery?

20.

Have you ever had a time when you had to concentrate on getting back on your feet? Were you at a financial or emotional loss? Did it take you long? Too long? How did you wait out your time? Were there times you thought the challenge was just too great?

21.

Have you ever had to take legal action against anybody, or had legal action taken against you? Was it rough? How did you get along with your lawyer? What was his office like?

22.

Do you often go to theater, concerts, or museums? Are you a patron of any cultural organization? Why are you involved with the ones you've chosen? Did you ever have a desire to be a performer?

23.

What magazines do you subscribe to? Which ones do you pick up at the drugstore or grocery? Do they tend to pile up on the floor beside your bed, or on the end table by your armchair? Are they the same magazines you've always read, or have they changed?

### 24.

Who takes care of money in your house? Where do you keep your checkbook? Do you sit in the same spot every month to take care of your household business, or do you plop down at the kitchen table when the spirit moves you?

### 25.

Who did you live with before you lived with your spouse? A roommate? Your parents? Another relative? Did you live in a walk-up apartment, a double house, or did you take a room somewhere?

### 26.

Do you enjoy watching daytime TV? Evening TV? Which shows do you find yourself tuning in to? Do you keep the television on regularly for company and noise in the house, or do you just turn it on to see a specific program?

### 27.

Do you subscribe to *TV Guide*? Do you do the crosswords? Do you read the horoscopes? Have you ever made any of the Kraft recipes featured around Super Bowl or holiday time?

### 28.
Has retirement been a positive or negative experience?

### 29.
Do you and your spouse enjoy the same hobbies? Have you taken up any new ones together, or are your individual hobbies valuable time apart for you?

### 30.
Do you enjoy a slower pace now, or find yourself as busy as ever?

### 31.
Have you met any new friends since you retired, or do you still pal around with the same old crowd?

### 32.
Do you—and did you—do most of the work around your house yourself, or do (did) you hire people to do it? The housework, say, or the yardwork. Are you a putterer?

### 33.

How much time do you spend with your grandkids?

### 34.

Did you ever have to help one of your friends, or your spouse, through a family member's illness or death?

# POLITICS AND HISTORY

### 1.

Which president did you admire most in your lifetime? Which president who lived before your time?

### 2.

Do you have a strong political party alliance? Have you ever worked on a campaign? Have you ever worked at a polling place?

### 3.

Which domestic problems are utmost in your town today? How have you noticed them firsthand? Do homeless people populate the library or the doughnut shop? Are there a lot fewer help-wanted ads in the classified section of the newspaper than there used to be?

### 4.

Where do you go to vote? The elementary school? A neighbor's house? Do you see the same people there every year?

### 5.

What have been your causes over the years? How have you worked for them? What do you do about the issues that bother you? Volunteer work? Charitable donations?

### 6.

Did you ever wear campaign buttons or use bumper stickers? Which campaign slogans stick in your mind? Which ones do you remember from your growing up?

### 7.

Have you ever found yourself going against popular opinion or beliefs politically? Has this caused you any problems?

### 8.

How have you seen racial injustice firsthand? Have you ever been the target of prejudice?

### 9.

What do you see as our country's most pressing problem today?

### 10.

Is there a government policy that you strongly disagree with? Do you think the welfare system is run correctly? Are your Social Security benefits what you think they should be?

### 11.

Do you follow local goings-on in city government? Are you on first-name terms with any of the local politicians? Are they bright and knowledgeable? Are they as capable as the people who used to run local government?

### 12.

Has there been a case of corruption or scandal that has rocked your town? Were you surprised when it came to light?

### 13.

Did you ever run for office? Did you win? How did you campaign?

### 14.

Have you ever been on jury duty? What was the case? Did you decide the defendant guilty or innocent? Was it a hard judgment call? Did it keep you awake nights?

### 15.

Did you personally know anyone victimized during the McCarthy era? Where did you live at the time?

What was it like to watch the Army-McCarthy hearings on TV?

### 16.

What have your feelings been about the space program? Where were you when Neil Armstrong walked on the moon?

### 17.

Do you own a flag? Do you display it?

### 18.

Did you build a bomb shelter? How did you supply it? What cans of food did you put down there? What kind of bottled water and other beverages? What kind of paper goods?

### 19.

Do you mostly vote for losers or winners?

### 20.

Where were you when you heard about Pearl Harbor?

### 21.

Did you like Ike?

### 22.

Did you have loved ones in Vietnam? Did they all come back? Do you see, in them, any of the damage that war can do?

### 23.

Did you ever march for or against anything? Was this acceptable to your family? What finally made you decide to take your stance?

### 24.

What did you think of Operation Desert Storm?

### 25.

Where were you when Franklin Roosevelt died? When John Kennedy was shot? Robert Kennedy? Martin Luther King?

### 26.

Name a *Life* magazine cover you especially remember. A *Time* magazine cover. A *Look* magazine cover.

### 27.

Do you feel the same way about politics and politicians as you did when you first became old enough to vote?

### 28.

What do you think was America's grandest national moment during your lifetime? America's lowest national moment?

### 29.

Is there a time in history you think it would have been fascinating to live in? Why?

### 30.

Have you ever seen a president in person? Where? What was it like?

### 31.

What direction do you think the country is going in today? Are you optimistic or pessimistic about the nation's future?

### 32.

What was it like keeping up with world events before the advent of television? Did the bad news of the world seem farther away? Slower moving? Less, or more, frightening?

### 33.

How does being an American feel different from the way it felt forty years ago?

# $\mathcal{Y}$OUR COMMUNITY
ை

### 1.

How would you describe your community? Rural? Suburban? Urban? What about your state? Deep South? Midwest? Northeast?

### 2.

Are there mountains where you live? Lakes? A river? Beachfront? Did you ice skate on the lake or canoe down the river?

### 3.

What is the big business in the town you live in now? What was the big business in the town you grew up in? Did you know any of the community leaders? Did you become one?

### 4.

Are there major highways going through your town? What is the nearest airport? Have you spent much time there? How do people get to the airport in your town? Cab? Bus? Shuttle? Or is it close in enough that relatives and friends drop off and pick up one another?

### 5.

Which public buildings do you use? The library? The municipal swimming pool? Town tennis courts?

### 6.

What are your local newspapers? Has your name ever been mentioned in one? Has your picture ever appeared? How did you feel about all of that?

### 7.

Was there a heavily delineated rich side of town and poor side of town? Did you spend much time in one or the other?

### 8.

Do you use public transportation? Is it decent and fairly easy to use? Is it safe? How much does it cost? Where do you catch it? Where are you dropped off? What do you think about the drivers?

### 9.

Have you ever had any dealings with the local police or firefighters? Have you had friends or relatives on the force? Which stations do you drive by most regularly? What kind of action do you notice going on there?

### 10.

Is there a local parade every year, or an annual festival? Are there any amusement parks or other tourist draws? Do you have a fair there? What time of year does it happen? What foods do you eat at the fair?

### 11.

Did you ever win a stuffed animal at a game booth at the fair?

### 12.

Which buildings do you think of when you think about downtown? How would you describe the skyline? Have you seen it change over the years?

### 13.

What is the big department store where you live? Have most of the shoppers moved to malls? Indoor or outdoor malls? Do you go there often? What shops are there? Did you prefer shopping downtown?

### 14.

Who is your most famous local celebrity? Who are your newscasters? Do you have any local business people who have funny or ridiculous commercials on TV?

### 15.

Was there ever a crime spree in your town that you remember particularly well? Was the criminal caught? How did the community react?

### 16.

Is there one most popular park in your town? Did you used to go there? Do you go there still?

### 17.

Has any area of town been gentrified and changed very much since you've lived there? Do you remember it the way it was before? Which do you prefer?

### 18.

What is the most popular steak house in town? The most popular seafood restaurant? Chinese restaurant? Pizza joint?

### 19.

Do any of the areas of your town have picturesque names? Colonial Village, Dogtown, Moon Heights?

### 20.

How many different parts of your town have you lived in? Why did you move?

### 21.

What is the best school system in your community? Did you go there? Did your kids go there?

### 22.

What are your local sports? Do you have a pro team?

### 23.

Is there much of a problem with homelessness in your town? Are the social services agencies effective? Do you think things used to be this way, but people back then dealt with such matters differently?

### 24.

Have you ever been to your city hall or municipal court building? Was it a good experience or bad?

### 25.

Does your town have a famous statue or sculpture? Do you like it or hate it?

### 26.

Is there a true community center in town, or does each ethnic or religious group have one of its own? Where do people truly gather? At the mall? Or do they gather at all?

### 27.

When out-of-towners think about your town, what do they think of? Your football team? Your famous clam chowder? Your supposedly crooked politicians? Skiing your mountains?

### 28.

How far is it to the nearest big city? How often do you go there? What for? Theater? Shopping? How do you get there? Do you go there as often as you used to?

### 29.

What is the most well-known painting in your local museum? Have you ever seen it? What other artwork do you enjoy looking at in the same museum?

### 30.

Where does the circus stop when it comes to town?

### 31.

Do you have loved ones buried in the cemetery in town? Do you visit? Is it maintained to your satisfaction?

### 32.

Are you more afraid to walk around at night in your community than you used to be?

### 33.

Are you able to hear any public events—a football game, the fireworks—from the quiet of your backyard at night?

# YOUR HOUSE NOW

### 1.

What is different about your home now from the home you raised your family in? If you decided to move from the family home, what was the deciding factor?

### 2.

What do you like about where you live now? What do you dislike about it? Is there something about this home that you've always wanted in a home?

### 3.

How did you feel each time you moved? Was it a hello or a good-bye?

### 4.

What is the quirkiest aspect of your house? Enclosed stairs to an attic? A lavatory under the stairs?

### 5.

Is it a one-story, two-story? Wood, stone, or brick? Do you have a frontyard, a sideyard, a backyard?

### 6.

What kinds of things do you have hanging on your refrigerator door? Do you have a laundry room? Does your house have any of the old-fashioned amenities: a broom closet, a cupboard just for trays, a breakfast room?

### 7.

If you've moved to a condominium or to an apartment, was that a difficult decision? Why did you do it? Do you have other friends in the complex? Ones you've met there, or ones you already knew?

### 8.

Do you have the kitchen you want? How would you change it?

### 9.

Do you have the bathroom you want? How would you change it?

### 10.

Would you rather have a luxurious kitchen or bathroom?

### 11.

What would you say your decorating style is? Did you redecorate when you moved, or did you make do with what you had? Do you have one item of furniture that has been with you in every home since your first?

### 12.

Which is the most comfortable room in your house? What do you spend time doing there?

### 13.

Is your living room formal, or do you actually use it? What does your couch look like? Do you ever fall asleep on it? Do you keep a throw blanket on it to use when you're reading or watching TV?

### 14.

Do you have a porch or a balcony that you sit on? Do you sit there in the morning, or in the evening? Where do you sit to read the paper? Where do you watch TV?

### 15.

Do you have any needlepoint sayings on a pillow or hanging on a wall?

### 16.

Do you have a gas stove, or electric? Do you use a microwave? Is your kitchen the kind of kitchen that is comfortable to sit around in?

### 17.

Do you have a favorite chair? Have you moved it from house to house with you? Where did you get it? When you bought it, did you sense that it would become your favorite?

### 18.

Have you ever had a feud with your neighbors? How did you resolve it?

### 19.

Do you spend much time in your bedroom, or do you go there only to sleep? Do you watch TV in bed, drink your coffee in bed, read the newspaper in bed? Do you make your bed every day?

### 20.

Where do you usually sit to make most of your phone calls? Do you have a portable phone? Do you do anything else while you're talking on it?

### 21.

Have you had any major home improvements done? Do you use the same repairmen over and over? Housepainters?

### 22.

What addition would you make to your house if you could?

### 23.

Do you have enough room for books in your house? Do you have one room that is primarily book-shelves? Are your shelves overflowing? What knick-knacks do you keep on the shelves?

### 24.

Where else do you have books? Piled beside your bed? Stacked up on a living room table? Where do you keep your magazines? Which ones do you sub-scribe to?

### 25.

What do you do with your old newspapers? Stack them on top of the refrigerator? Put them out in the garage? Recycle them?

### 26.

What kind of trees grow in your neighborhood? Is your yard shady? Is your home filled with light?

### 27.

What do you see from your kitchen window? From your bedroom window?

### 28.

Are there birds or squirrels in your yard? Raccoon or deer?

### 29.

What time does your mail come? Is your mailbox right at your door, or do you have to walk a ways to get it? Do you have your name on your mailbox?

### 30.

Where do you put your purse when you walk in the door? Where do you hang or place your keys?

### 31.

Do you park in your garage? Do you have a garage-door opener? Is your garage organized, or more of a messy storage space? What seasonal items do you keep out there and haul in when the time comes?

### 32.

Do you have the same table and chairs you had in the house where you raised your family? Have you had them refinished? Do you still sit at the same spot at the table as when you were raising your children?

### 33.
Is the house too quiet for you with the children gone? Or do you welcome the absence of commotion?

### 34.
Do you lock your door day and night? Did you have to thirty or forty years ago?

### 35.
What would your dream house be?

# EVERYDAY LIFE

### 1.

What have been the personal landmarks in your life? Did you turn at the Sunoco station when you were coming home from your errands? Was there a newsstand you stopped at frequently? What did you see every day on your route to school? To work?

### 2.

What grocery store do you use? Which is the first aisle you go down? How much does a usual trip to the store cost you? What grocery stores did you used to go to? Which was your favorite? Why?

### 3.

What drugstore do you go to? Do you know the pharmacist by name? What else do you chat about, other than your prescriptions?

### 4.

What drycleaner do you go to? Do you know the people who run it? Do they deliver? Do you get your clothes altered there? What is the dressing room like? What is the tailor's name?

### 5.

Do you use coupons?

### 6.

Do you like to watch the sun go down? What time do you get up in the morning?

### 7.

What part of housework do you hate most? How was it always split up in your family? Did the men generally do the outside work while the women took care of the inside? Did you ever have household help? Was that hard for you to get used to?

### 8.

What type of store do you like to browse in? Bookstores? Hardware stores? Cookware stores? Garden stores? Or do you hate shopping altogether?

### 9.

What's your daily routine? Do you get up, drink coffee, have a shower? Drink tea, go get the paper? Watch a morning television show, listen to a certain radio program, call a certain friend?

### 10.

How much did postage stamps cost when you began to be aware of such things?

### 11.

If you have been slowed any by age, which simple activities do you miss?

### 12.

Is there someone you talk with every day? Your sister? Your daughter? A best friend or neighbor?

### 13.

How do you spend your time outdoors? Gardening, yardwork? Just sitting, enjoying the air?

### 14.

What do your cooking implements look like? Your pots, your pans? What do the dishes you use look like? What about your coffeepot?

### 15.

Do you use an electric blanket or a quilt? Do you sleep in a twin bed, a double, a queen, a king? Do you use foam rubber or feather pillows? What do you keep on your nightstand?

### 16.

Do you shave with a razor, or with an electric shaver?

### 17.

Do you keep your old photos in an album or a shoebox? How often do you take them out and look at them?

### 18.

What beauty parlor or barber shop do you go to? What is your beautician or barber's name? Do you have a standing appointment? How often do you go there? What do you usually have done? A perm, color, a cut? A shave, or just a haircut? Do you ever get your nails done at the same time? What magazines do they have there for customers to read?

### 19.

What newspapers do you read? What nightly newscast do you watch? Local? National? Do you eat your dinner in front of the set or have your late snack there while you check out the news?

### 20.

Do you bathe, or do you shower? Did you decide between one or the other early in your life?

### 21.

Do you wash your dishes by hand or in a dishwasher?

### 22.

What does your robe look like? Your favorite nightgown or pajamas?

### 23.

What do you keep in your dresser drawers? Socks in top drawer, underthings in second drawer? Do you keep family pictures on the top of your dresser?

### 24.

What is your doctor's name? Your dentist? Have you gone to the same person for a while, or have you recently switched? If you have, why?

### 25.

Where is the mirror that you look at yourself in every day? Is it in the bedroom? In the bathroom? In the hall by the front door?

### 26.

Do you lunch with friends? Do you have dinner with them? Who drives?

### 27.

Do you read the letters to the editor in the newspaper? Have you ever written one? Was it published?

### 28.

What do you feed your dog? Your cat?

### 29.

What route do you take around your house at night before you finally turn in? Do you lock the door, chain it, set the timer on the coffeepot, turn on the light in the hall, brush your teeth, set the alarm? Are you ever too tired to do these things, or would you be unable to fall asleep if you didn't?

### 30.

What is the first thing you see when you open your eyes in the morning? What is the first thing that you think about? What is the last thing you see before turning out the lights at night? What do you think about while you're drifting off?

# HABITS

### 1.
Are you usually late or early?

### 2.
Are you more comfortable speaking or writing? Do you enjoy talking on the phone more than writing letters?

### 3.
Do you have any superstitions? Do you knock wood, throw salt over your shoulder, avoid black cats?

### 4.
Do you have certain days of the week when you do certain chores? Do you do washing on Monday, ironing on Tuesday, marketing on Wednesday, etc.?

### 5.
Did your parents read to you? Did you read to your children? Do they read to their children?

### 6.

Do you take your bath or shower in the morning or the evening? Do you sing in the shower?

### 7.

Do you garden? Vegetable or flower? What do you grow?

### 8.

What was the first thing you usually did when you came home from work? Read the mail, fixed a drink, answered phone calls, made dinner, watched a game show, watered the lawn, called your mom? Do you follow this same routine now? If not, how has it changed?

### 9.

What has been your exercise program? What was it when you were younger? Now? Have you ever belonged to a health club? Do you walk in your neighborhood or at the mall?

### 10.

Do you play the lottery? Have you ever won? Where do you buy your tickets? Which games do you play?

### 11.

Have you ever been addicted to anything? Did you work hard to lose the addiction? Was it much of a struggle?

### 12.

Do you like music on in the house, or silence? Do you turn on the TV for company?

### 13.

Do you eat your meals at the same time every day? Do you sit down at a table or in front of the TV? Do you use placemats if it's just you?

### 14.

What's your most comfortable at-home outfit? A sweatsuit? A ratty old robe? Old pants?

### 15.

Have you ever smoked cigarettes? What brand? What was their slogan? What did the package look like? How much did they cost? How much do they cost now? Where do you buy them? Do you wish you didn't smoke?

### 16.

Do you doodle? What figures tend to come up? Boxes? Circles? Faces?

### 17.

Are you a list maker?

### 18.

Is your calendar messy or neat? Where do you hang a calendar? On the back of your broom-closet door? Do you keep a desk or pocket calendar? Do you buy the same kind every year?

### 19.

Do you use a dictionary? Do you keep it by your chair, or up on the bookshelf?

### 20.

When someone sneezes, do you say "Gesundheit," or "God bless you"? Do you have other sayings that just naturally come out of your mouth?

### 21.

What is your bedtime ritual? Do you read before going to sleep or watch a late-night talk show?

### 22.

Do you do the crossword puzzles in the newspaper? When? In the morning or evening? Where do you usually sit to do them?

### 23.

Do you read the Bible, or a daily meditation book? Where do you keep it? Beside your bed? Did somebody special give it to you? Did somebody special teach you about its importance?

### 24.

Do you have a habit you'd like to break? How about one you'd like to start?

### 25.

Does anyone you know have a particularly annoying habit?

### 26.

What is the first thing you turn to in the newspaper? The sports section? The funnies? The horoscope? In which order do you read the paper? Which magazine do you try not to miss?

### 27.

Where is the desk in your house? What do you do there? Pay the bills? Talk on the phone? Write letters?

### 28.

Is watching the evening news part of your routine? Even on the weekends?

### 29.

What kind of toothpaste do you use? Do you floss?

### 30.

What do you do in the first hour after you wake up each morning?

### 31.

In what order do you keep your currency in your wallet?

### 32.

What do you do with your pocket change at the end of the day?

### 33.

Do you keep an ear out for the mail carrier? Do you open personal mail before bills or mass mailings, or do you save the personal mail for last?

### 34.

Is there somewhere in town you stop every day?
Every week?

---

### 35.

Do you make New Year's resolutions? Did you
when you were younger?

### 36.

Do you buy in bulk?

# APPEARANCES

**1.**

Describe what you look like now. Have you been happy with the way you look? What did you look like as a teenager? As a young child?

**2.**

If you had to name a famous person whom you looked like, who would it be?

**3.**

Who would you most like to look like?

**4.**

Has your appearance played an important part in your getting along in the world? Has it been detrimental or beneficial, do you think?

**5.**

What is your best feature? Your worst? Do you have any birthmarks or scars that differentiate your looks absolutely from anyone else you know?

6.

Have you ever considered plastic surgery? If so, did you end up doing it? If not, why not? Moral opposition, financial considerations, or just plain fear?

7.

In your heart of hearts, are you vain? Have you ever been oversensitive about the way you look, or has it been of little import to you?

8.

What would you change about your appearance, if it could be done magically and not surgically? Do you wish you were taller or shorter or built bigger and stronger?

9.

What did you think of the long hair so popular in the sixties? Did it offend your sensibilities, or did you grow your own and sport sideburns? Did your son or daughter affect the so-called hippie look? Was this OK with you, or were you appalled?

10.

Who do you look most like in your family? Is there a family look, would you say, making your kin recognizable all the way down the line?

### 11.

Have you ever had any facial hair? Did you try different styles of mustaches and beards? Did you like the way you looked? Did your wife like it, too? How long did you keep it? And what precipitated the change?

### 12.

What color is/was your hair? Is it curly or straight, thick or thin? Have you spent much time taking care of it over the years? Too much time, do you think?

### 13.

How tall are you? Were you tall or short for your age? Too much so, in your opinion? Was it a big deal to you? Were you self-conscious?

### 14.

What is your most comfortable outfit? What outfit do you think you look best in? How about when you were younger?

### 15.

Is there something you remember particularly well that you wore to high school? To college classes? To college weekends? To elementary school?

### 16.

What fashion trends have you seen come and go? Pantsuits, middie blouses, stretch pants, leisure suits? Did you own any of these? Did you follow the trends? Was one of them right for you—particularly flattering?

### 17.

Do you remember getting your first suit and tie? Your first nylons and heels?

### 18.

Do you prefer big purses or small pocketbooks? Do you have an evening bag that you are very fond of? What events have you carried it to? What do you keep in it? A compact, lipstick, and a comb?

### 19.

What color lipstick do you wear; eye shadow, nail polish?

### 20.

Do you tan or burn?

### 21.

Are you a conventional dresser? Were you always? What did your parents think about what you wore?

### 22.

What jewelry do you wear? A wedding band? A pin of your mother's? A watch of your father's? A charm bracelet? Where did you get the charms? Did somebody special give you some of them for an anniversary or your birthday? Do you wear anything that represents your children or grandkids?

### 23.

Have you ever worn hats?

### 24.

What kind of shoes are you partial to?

### 25.

Have you ever worn a uniform?

### 26.

Were you upset when you first noticed signs of aging? When did this happen? With the first gray hairs, or lines around your eyes, or what?

### 27.

As a teenager, did you have skin problems? Was this traumatic for you?

28.

What preventive measures do you take to care for the way you look? Sun block? Face cream?

29.

Have you ever had your ears pierced? Where did you go to do it? Who went with you? What were the first earrings you bought yourself after you had this done?

30.

What athletic shoes do you prefer?

31.

Do you like to wear ties? If you didn't have to, would you? What kinds are your favorites?

32.

Are you a creature of habit, wearing variations of the same look every day? Or do you enjoy switching your outfits dramatically?

33.

Do your children look like you, or like your spouse?

# GRANDPARENTHOOD

### 1.

Where were you when your child told you that you were going to be a grandparent? What were your first words?

### 2.

Who called you from the hospital to tell you your first grandchild was born? What time was it? Who was the first person you called?

### 3.

Were you able to go see the new family in the hospital? Did you take a gift? What did you think the first minute the nurse brought the baby to the room?

### 4.

Were you able to go over to the house much and help out with the new baby? Did you cook dinner for the new family or bathe the baby? Did you stay over, or come and go in the mornings and evenings?

### 5.

When did your grandchild first say your name? Were you at your house or at the child's house? What do your grandchildren call you?

### 6.

Did you ever make anything by hand for your grandchild? A needlepoint pillow? A wooden toy? A quilt? Did you enjoy shopping for the baby? What clothes did you buy? What toys did you buy?

### 7.

Did you baby-sit often? At their house? At your house? Do you have a special room for the grandchildren at your house? What toys do you keep there?

### 8.

Do you enjoy taking your grandchildren out for meals in restaurants? What is their favorite place? What do they like to order?

### 9.

Have you ever taken your grandchildren on a trip with you? One at a time, or in a group? Were you satisfied with the way these trips turned out?

### 10.

What souvenirs did you bring your grandchildren from your travels? Do any of your grandchildren have a collection that you keep adding to?

### 11.

How would you discipline your grandchildren differently from the way their parents do? What do they do that drives you crazy? How would you have fixed that?

### 12.

Do your grandchildren ever come spend the night with you? How do you spend those evenings?

### 13.

Do your grandchildren look like your own children did as babies? Do they have similar temperament? Do you ever miss the days when you had babies of your own?

### 14.

When your grandchildren leave your house from visiting you, are you sorry, or are you pretty exhausted?

### 15.

What presents have you given them over the years? Did you attend their birthday parties where their friends came, or did you celebrate with just the family?

### 16.

Do you know any of your grandchildren's friends? Are you comfortable with them? Do they visit at your house with your grandchildren?

### 17.

Have you taught your grandchildren any games or hobbies? Do you play cards with them? Have you taught them needlepoint or cooking? Do you bake with them?

### 18.

What do you fix your grandchildren to eat when they come visit you?

### 19.

What do your grandchildren's rooms look like? What do they have hanging on the walls? Do they have bunk beds or twin beds? What do their bedspreads look like?

20.

What do you call your grandchildren? Do you have nicknames for them?

21.

Can you see your face anywhere in your grand-child's face?

22.

How are your grandchildren on the phone? Are they fairly communicative, or can you hardly coax the words out of their mouths?

23.

What television shows do you and your grandchil-dren watch together? Have you gone to the movies together? A play? A circus?

24.

Can you recall one especially memorable thing each of your grandchildren has said?

25.

Do you have their artwork hanging on your walls or put up with magnets on your refrigerator door? Have they ever made you anything out of clay? Where do you keep it?

### 26.

How does family life differ for your grandchildren from the way family life was for you?

### 27.

What are your wishes for your grandchildren?

### 28.

Do you truly trust that the world will be a decent place for their growing up?

### 29.

What one thing would you like to be sure they remember?

### 30.

What do you want them to remember about you?

### 31.

Do you ever sense that your grandchildren are not especially eager to visit you, and would rather be with their friends? Does this hurt your feelings, or do you remember feeling the same way on visits to your own grandparents?

### 32.

What is the best part of being a grandparent? The worst?

### 33.

What does it feel like five minutes after your grandchildren have left your house?

### 34.

How easy is it for you to resist telling your children how to raise your grandchildren? Have you ever had a tense or unpleasant discussion with your children about this subject?

### 35.

Which is better—being a parent or a grandparent?

### 36.

If you could be your grandchildren's age today, would you?

# TRAVELS AND LEISURE TIME

## 1.

What did you always like best about the weekends? Did you have a usual routine: Friday night pizza and movies; Saturday chores; Saturday night dinner out? Or did you take various getaways? Go for long drives? Visit friends or relatives in other towns?

## 2.

What do you like best about weekends now? Do the streets seem busier with working people out doing chores? Do you now save your errands for weekdays? Do you still allow more flexibility in your life on the weekends, even though you may be retired?

## 3.

What does your luggage look like? Where did you get it? When? Was luggage a "big gift" to you for any occasion? Did you get new luggage to go away to college, or to start your married life?

## 4.

Did you ever pack a trunk?

### 5.

Have you ever gone to Europe? Other overseas travel? Would you like to?

### 6.

Where do you like to go on vacation? To the beach? To a tourist town? To a national park?

### 7.

Is there a certain time of year when you always take your trips? Do you find yourself heading to Florida in March, to Arizona in December?

### 8.

Is there any place you've been that you'd really like to visit again? Which restaurant do you hope is still there? Would you try to stay at the same hotel? What was it about that place that would draw you again—the physical beauty of the surroundings, or a happy memory of a personal time?

### 9.

Do you vacation, still, with your children and grandchildren? Do you meet at a special spot you've gone to over the years? Is it a family cabin, a Florida beach, a family member's house?

10.

When your children were growing up, did you always take them along on vacation, or were there times when you could get away by yourselves? Who stayed with the kids? How often did you phone home? What important things do you remember happening to one of them while you were away?

11.

When you went on family vacations, did the kids play games in the car? How crazy did they drive you, asking, "Are we there yet?" Did everyone bundle into a motel room together, or were kids in one room, you in the other?

12.

What was the most beautiful hotel room you ever stayed in? What did you see out the windows? What amenities dazzled you? Did you order room service there? Why were you in that town, that time?

13.

Have you ever camped? What is it about camping that you liked—or didn't like? Did you own the equipment or borrow it? Did you camp out with another family?

### 14.

What are your campfire treats?

### 15.

Do you get homesick? What talismans do you bring from home—which touchstones to make yourself feel more connected?

### 16.

Where did you go on your honeymoon? Why there? How did you get to your destination? How long did you stay?

### 17.

Are you a souvenir buyer? Do you go for the junk, or for the specialty items a region is known for? Have you ever gone on a trip with shopping as the main reason? Have you gone to places known for pottery, places known for silk, places known for fine leather goods, so you'll come back with some?

### 18.

What are some souvenirs you remember? What special thing did you ever bring back from a trip for someone else?

### 19.

Do you take pictures on vacation? What kind of camera do you use? Are you generally pleased with the way the pictures turn out? Have you ever asked a passerby to take a picture of you? Do you have any pictures of you on vacation displayed in your house?

### 20.

What was your splurgiest vacation? Did you ever go somewhere you really could not afford to go just because you wanted to so much? Is there somewhere still that you would like to visit? Are you making plans to get there?

### 21.

Who have been your traveling companions? Did you and your spouse ever travel with other couples? What is the key to getting along on a trip?

### 22.

Have you always been glad to get home?

### 23.

Have you ever taken a trip alone? Would you like that? Did you ever take time off from your family and travel with a friend?

### 24.

Have you and your spouse always agreed about the way to spend leisure time? What if one of you liked the mountains and the other liked the seaside? Did you alternate, compromise, or did one of you acquiesce?

### 25.

Have you met anyone on vacation whom you continued to correspond with? Do you have "same time, next year" friends? What is it about them that you like? Have they ever visited you in your hometown? Was that sort of strange—seeing them on your home turf, away from the vacation atmosphere?

### 26.

Do you remember going on any trips with your parents? Did you try to make the ones you took with your own kids similar experiences, or far different ones?

### 27.

Do you miss train travel? What was it about a passenger train that was better than air travel? In what ways is air travel better?

### 28.

What was your first train trip with your parents like? Your first train trip by yourself?

### 29.

Did you ever sleep in a train's sleeper car? What was that like?

### 30.

How would you compare the feeling of a big train station to the feeling of a big airport?

### 31.

When was your first time in an airplane? Do you like to fly? Do you plan your trips around airlines' specials?

### 32.

Do you use a travel agent, or arrange your own trips?

### 33.

Which airport do you find yourself in the most when traveling? How has it changed over the years? Is it full of shops and foodstands? Is there something you like to get or see there every time you pass through?

### 34.
Where is the most exotic place you've ever been?

### 35.
Have you ever gotten sick while on vacation?

### 36.
Have you ever been to a World's Fair?

### 37.
When a vacation trip ends, are you usually ready to go home—or do you wish it could last longer? Is there "no place like home"?

# VEHICLES

### 1.

What are you driving now? How many years have you had your car?

### 2.

When did you get your first car? Did you buy it for yourself or did your parents help you? Where did you get it; off a lot or from a private party? How much did you pay? How did you earn the money?

### 3.

Were you in love with the car? Did you give it a nickname? Where did you take it on the first spin? Who were the first people you gave rides to? Which people drove around in that car with you the most?

### 4.

How much did a tank of gas cost in those days? Where did you usually fill up?

### 5.

What color was your first bike? When did you get it? Was it all that you imagined a two-wheeler to be?

### 6.

Who taught you to ride the bike? Did you ever take a serious fall?

### 7.

Can you remember having a tricycle, or other backyard vehicle? What kind of bikes did your siblings have? Did you ride together?

### 8.

Did you ever ride a tandem bike?

### 9.

Were you ever tempted to get a motorcycle?

### 10.

Do you have a vanity license plate? Did you ever? Would you ever? Do any of your friends have them? What do you think about vanity plates?

### 11.

What is your dream car? Did you ever own it? How important was it to you? If money were not an issue, would you buy it still?

### 12.

Who taught you to drive? What was that like? Were you intimidated? Did you learn on a stick shift?

### 13.

Where did you test for your driver's license? Did you get it the first time out?

### 14.

Have you ever put a bumper sticker on your car? Was it one touting a political candidate, or a funny phrase, or a slogan for a cause you uphold?

### 15.

What do you listen to when you are in your car? The radio? Tapes? Quiet? The world through your open windows?

### 16.

What's your favorite driving song?

### 17.

Do you prefer driving with your windows open or with the air conditioner on?

### 18.

What do you keep in your glove compartment? Do you carry any safety items, or just Kleenex and such?

### 19.

After you learned to drive, did you think it was all it was cracked up to be? Do you still get a kick out of it?

### 20.

Have you ever spent time on a boat or taken a cruise?

### 21.

Do you have a license to drive anything other than an automobile? A plane? A motorcycle?

### 22.

Have you ever operated heavy machinery?

### 23.

Do you feel you drive as well as you ever did? Or have you given up your license? If so, was that hard on you?

### 24.

Are you an aggressive or a defensive driver?

### 25.

Do you prefer automatic or standard shift?

### 26.

What kind of gas do you use? How much does it cost you to fill up? Do you pump your own or go for full service? Why?

### 27.

Is it important to you to buy an American automobile? Have your feelings about that changed over the years?

### 28.

Are you brand-loyal? Have you repeatedly bought Fords or Chevies? Are you model-loyal? Have you ever owned a string of Thunderbirds or Lincoln Town Cars or Bonnevilles?

### 29.

Have you ever changed a tire, changed your oil, repaired your engine or brakes yourself?

### 30.

Do you belong to AAA? Does your car always start in the winter?

### 31.

Have you ever been in an automobile accident? What were the circumstances? Were you hurt? Was your passenger hurt? Was driving more nerve-wracking after that?

### 32.

Do you enjoy road trips?

### 33.

Have any of your cars been lemons?

### 34.

Are today's new cars as enticing to you, or do they all look the same? Do you pay much attention to the new models when they are announced?

### 35.

What is the fastest you have ever driven?

### 36.

Are other motorists on the roads these days more or less courteous than when you were first driving? What changes in people's driving etiquette have you noticed?

### 37.

What was it like when the interstate highway system was built? How did this change the feel of driving? The feel of America?

### 38.

Was it difficult for you to get used to the idea of driving on freeways?

### 39.

Did you ever like to just drive around aimlessly—"cruise"—either by yourself or with friends? Do you ever do that still?

### 40.

What is the best drive you have ever taken? What made it so good?

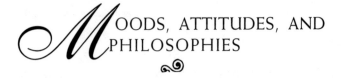

# MOODS, ATTITUDES, AND PHILOSOPHIES

*1.*

Do you like rainy days? What do you do on them?

2.

As an "old dog," have you learned new tricks? Can you use a computer? Would you want to?

3.

What heroic attributes do you have? What not-so-heroic-at-all attitudes do you have?

*4.*

Would you say you're a doer or a procrastinator?

5.

Would you say you're lucky?

6.

Do you get angry in traffic? Do you mutter at your fellow motorists?

### 7.

Have you been able to trust most of your instincts? Did you ever follow instinct instead of logic or judgment? How did it work out?

### 8.

Are you afraid to cry? Are you a pretty good fighter?

### 9.

What makes you angry?

### 10.

How do you handle being deeply upset?

### 11.

What are you like when you're sick? Do you like to be taken care of or left alone?

### 12.

Are you afraid of doctors?

### 13.

What's your pet peeve? Do you tell smokers not to smoke around you? Do you tell someone if her perfume is bothering you?

### 14.

Do you consider yourself lazy?

### 15.

Are you patient or impatient?

### 16.

Are you a jealous person?

### 17.

Do you have a tendency to get the blues? Did anyone else in your family? Does there seem to be a dominant personality trait in your family? Are you hotheads? Do you avoid conflict? Are you worriers? Are you hypochondriacs?

### 18.

What behavior can you simply not abide?

### 19.

Are you easy or difficult to get along with?

### 20.

What character trait have you seen in someone else that you would like to have had?

### 21.

Would you say you've lived in the moment, or dwelled too much on the future or the past?

### 22.

Would you rather live near the mountains or the sea? Are you a city mouse or a country mouse?

### 23.

Who is your hero?

### 24.

Do you like to be alone?

### 25.

Would you say you have a philosophy of life?

### 26.

Do you believe in God or another higher power? Do you pray? Where do you do your worshipping?

### 27.

Do you believe in astrology, numerology, or any other alternative beliefs? Do you read your horoscope in the paper? Have you ever gone to a psychic?

### 28.

What do you think makes the world go round? What makes it go round for you?

### 29.

Is there something you believed for a long time that you don't believe anymore? What changed your mind?

### 30.

Do you ever bend the rules?

### 31.

Are you a dreamer, or a realist?

### 32.

Do you believe in an afterlife?

### 33.

What do you consider a necessary evil?

### 34.

Do you believe in nature, or nurture?

### 35.

How do you feel about buying on credit? Have you ever gotten yourself into trouble that way?

### 36.

How private are you? Do you live with an open-door policy, or is your home your private sanctuary? Do your friends call before they stop by?

### 37.

Do you have someone you confide in, or do you keep your troubles to yourself? Who comes to you with their troubles? How do you think you help them?

### 38.

What season of the year makes you the happiest?

# LOOKING BACK, OR 20/20 HINDSIGHT

## 1.
What was your favorite year? What was your favorite age?

## 2.
What is the most important date in your personal history?

## 3.
What do you think other people think of you? Do you think they see you the way you really are?

## 4.
What was the hardest thing that you ever had to do?

## 5.
What has been the angriest you've ever been? What did you do about it?

## 6.
How have you seen prices change over the years? Have you had a struggle being able to afford the

things you want and need? Have you ever felt wealthy?

### 7.

What was the first funeral you attended? How did it affect you? What was the last one you went to? Are they getting easier or harder?

### 8.

When do you first remember feeling like an adult? Did it come early or late in life?

### 9.

What fads have you seen come and go?

### 10.

Did you have definite goals? Did you achieve them? Are you still working on them? Any new ones?

### 11.

Did you have a year of living dangerously?

### 12.

When you really think about your childhood, was it completely carefree, or did you have your worries even then?

### 13.

Were you the same person you are now when you were a child, or were you very much different?

### 14.

Can you summarize where your family has been, and where it looks like it's going?

### 15.

What was your biggest mistake?

### 16.

Have you ever sent or received a telegram?

### 17.

Have you ever had a medical scare?

### 18.

Is there anything you would have done completely differently?

### 19.

If you could change anything in your life, what would you change?

### 20.

Do you like your name? If you could, would you choose another? What name would you choose?

### 21.

Is there anything you wish you had done, but didn't? Do you think you might still do it?

### 22.

If you had all the time in the world, what would you do?

### 23.

If you could look into the future, would you?

### 24.

If you could not be you, who would you be?

### 25.

What haven't you had enough of in your life? Time? Money? Love? Freedom?

### 26.

Have you experienced a natural disaster? An earthquake? A flood? How was your family affected?

### 27.

What's the biggest bargain you ever bought? What did you spend way too much on? What was your most foolish purchase?

### 28.

If, when you were a child, you had been able to look ahead and see your whole life right up to today, would you have been pleased with what you saw?

### 29.

Was there one moment in your life that changed everything for you?

### 30.

Have you ever been in the right place at the right time?

# HARD QUESTIONS: EXTRA CREDIT

1.

Who do you trust?

2.

Do you have any real vices?

3.

Is there anyone you envy? Why?

4.

Have you thought about what you want your epitaph to read?

5.

Do you want to be buried or cremated? Where would you like your ashes? Would you like a Viking funeral out at sea?

6.

What big things do you regret? Was there a turn in the road you think you should have taken?

### 7.

What little things do you regret? Did you buy a Ford when you should have bought a Chevy?

### 8.

Have you ever been a victim of crime? Ever committed a crime?

### 9.

Have you ever tried to do something right that backfired on you?

### 10.

Do you have a character trait that you'd like to give up? Are you selfish or timid? Is there a character trait that you'd like to pass on? Would you like your descendants to have your sense of humor or your knowledge of what's right?

### 11.

Have you ever had a feud that went on too long with anyone? Is there someone you just do not get along with?

### 12.

Do you feel that you put enough energy into parenting as you should have? Did you have energy left to take care of your parents in their older years?

### 13.

Do you have any fears or phobias? Have they changed during your life? How much have they affected you?

### 14.

What was your proudest moment: something that you did—not your child, not your spouse. Did you ever win an award for doing your job well, or for doing good work in your community? Or was it something you did privately, something that no one else knew about? How did you mark the experience for yourself?

### 15.

What person affected your life the most?

### 16.

Which sense would you regret losing the most? Have you lost any sharpness in any of them yet? Do you need to wear a hearing aid? Do you fear when that day comes?

### 17.

What was your biggest challenge? Was there something that you just did not want to do but had to go ahead and do anyway? How did it turn out for you? Were you victorious?

### 18.

Have you ever had a lucky charm? Do you wear it or carry it? Where did you get it? Did you find it on the street? How did you know this was the charm for you? Has it worked?

### 19.

Have you ever been witness to something that you can't forget? An act of courage, an act of violence, a natural landscape, a surprise in the dark?

### 20.

Have you had a reoccurring dream throughout your life? What do you think it means?

### 21.

What do you think is funny?

### 22.

What do you find yourself daydreaming about?

### 23.

Do you remember a time when you were acutely embarrassed?

### 24.

Do you like jokes? What's your favorite joke?

### 25.

If you got a tattoo, what would it be? Where?

### 26.

List your responsibilities.

### 27.

Have you ever felt betrayed?

### 28.

What are you proudest of about yourself?

### 29.

Have your moments of happiness outweighed your moments of regret?

### 30.

If you hold a fundamental truth, what is it?

# To Our Readers

You've asked yourselves a lot of questions during the course of writing your family history. Now we wonder whether you could take the time to answer one for us.

Here it is:

If you had to write a note—one note—and leave it propped against the sugar bowl on your kitchen table for future generations to read, what would you say in that note?

It might be a bit of philosophy you've learned over the years; it might be a helpful tip or piece of guidance. It might be a thought about the meaning of your life; it might be your most heartfelt wishes for the people who read it. Intimate or humorous, it can be anything you want.

One note—one note to leave in the kitchen, for your children's children, and theirs, and all of ours.

If you could write that note—it can be as short or as long as you wish—and share it with us, we will try to gather a collection of these thoughts for a future volume. You can mail a copy of your note to:

Note on the Kitchen Table
P.O. Box 90035-0035
Pasadena, California 91109

Thanks. We look forward to hearing from you.

# ABOUT THE AUTHORS

BOB GREENE is a syndicated columnist for the *Chicago Tribune*. His column appears in more than two hundred newspapers in the United States, Canada, and Japan. For nine years his "American Beat" was the lead column in *Esquire* magazine; as a broadcast journalist he has served as contributing correspondent for "ABC News Nightline." He is the author of twelve previous books, including *Hang Time*, *Be True to Your School*, and *Good Morning, Merry Sunshine*. His first novel, *All Summer Long*, will be published by Doubleday in 1993.

D. G. FULFORD is a columnist for the *Los Angeles Daily News*. Her columns are distributed nationally by the New York Times News Service. She is Bob Greene's sister.